Her Words ✍

HER WORDS

An Anthology of Poetry about the Great Goddess

⊰⊱

EDITED BY

BURLEIGH MUTÉN

SHAMBHALA
Boston & London
1999

SHAMBHALA PUBLICATIONS, INC.
Horticultural Hall
300 Massachusetts Avenue
Boston, Massachusetts 02115
www.shambhala.com

9 8 7 6 5 4 3 2 1

FIRST EDITION
Printed in the United States of America
♾ This edition is printed on acid-free paper that meets the
American National Standards Institute z39.48 Standard.
Distributed in the United States by Random House, Inc.,
and in Canada by Random House of Canada Ltd.

LIBRARY OF CONGRESS CATALOGING-IN-PUBLICATION DATA
Her words: an anthology of poetry about the Great Goddess/
edited by Burleigh Mutén.—1st ed.
  p. cm.
ISBN 1-57062-473-9
1. Goddess religion Poetry.   2. Women and religion Poetry.
3. Goddesses Poetry,   4. Religious poetry.   I. Mutén, Burleigh.
PN6110.G59H47   1999   99-23172
808.81'9382912114—dc21   CIP

In memory of my mentor

ALICE MOVENA SMITH ALLEN

1913–1994

✍

CONTENTS

INTRODUCTION

I<small>T'S A BLESSING TO BE A WOMAN</small> at this millennial juncture. It's a blessing because we know what our mothers and grandmothers didn't know. Thanks to scientific sophistication in the information age, we know about the Paleolithic Great Goddess who nourished the physical and spiritual needs of the ancients thirty thousand years ago. We know that the source of spiritual authority in the Western world was female.

During the past century, the stories of Inanna—Queen of Heaven and Earth, First Daughter of the Moon and of the Morning and Evening Stars, Goddess of Love and War—were deciphered by cuneiformists, revealing a fertile and ferocious goddess who was revered in the Middle East four thousand years ago. The Goddess of Willendorf, a rotund female figure that fits in the hand, was unearthed in Austria in 1908 and dated as thirty thousand years old. Thousands of Neolithic and Paleolithic female figures have been found in caves, tombs, and temples throughout Europe and Asia. Carved in bone, horn, and stone, these icons inform us of an age in which the female blood rites of menstruation, childbirth, and menopause were sacred.

As women's spiritual history has been uncovered during the late twentieth century, women all over Earth have once again found an authentic relationship to the Divine. The Great Goddess, Mother of All, Oldest of the Old, has returned to our conscious minds. She sits in our psyches. She rests in our hearts. She is an external force of Nature and an inner spark of divine knowledge. She recalls our kinship to the stars, to our planet, and to every living creature. She invokes our inner dignity. As the source of all creativity, she breathes into us, inspiring us to give birth to ourselves. Some of us, of course, do this through the written word.

As we write about the Lady of Ten Thousand Names, we are

reclaiming a relationship to our own divine feminine energy. We are identifying with potent female archetypes that validate the natural seasons of our own lives as maidens, mothers, and crones. As we write about Her, we are vessels holding the divine breath, inspired and enlivened by the sacred force of Nature we call Goddess. When we write, we hear Her voice.

Ten years ago, right after I discovered the concept of feminine deity, I read the Homeric "Hymn to Demeter" with new eyes. How could a goddess whose creative power brought the seasons and the gift of grain not know what had happened to her daughter? If she was a goddess, why wouldn't her intuition and her divine wisdom help her find her child? How could the daughter, a goddess herself, have been kidnapped to begin with? This story was as implausible to me as the Judeo-Christian god of my childhood. As I considered this, I heard the first line of a poem in my head. It was the first poem I'd written in years. It was the voice of a goddess preparing her daughter for her journey to the underworld, to the world of her own sexuality. It was the voice of a mother empowering her daughter. As the mystery of creation flowed through me, my fingers flew over the keys and "Demeter's Blessing" wrote itself. It was clear: a divine force had passed through me, the voice of the Goddess. Not long afterward, within a few months, my own adolescent daughter opened to her sexuality. I was strengthened by the model of a goddess who prepared her daughter for these rites.

Her Words spans the ages from the hymns to Inanna through biblical verses about Sophia and the works of sixth-century-BCE poet Sappho to the poetry of twentieth-century authors—Janine Canan, Lucille Clifton, Diane di Prima, Susan Griffin, Patricia Monaghan, May Sarton, Starhawk, Alma Luz Villanueva, and many others. Rather than break the poetry into two categories, past and present, I have interspersed ancient and modern verse. I did this because women's spirituality embraces a concept of cyclical, circular time rather than a linear order and because I found it fascinating to see the connections modern poets are making with the ancient archetypes.

Many of these poets re-vision the era in which women were sacred. Some recognize themselves in the archetypal icons, bringing ancient voices to twentieth-century dynamics. Some simply own the inner dignity and celebration of self that comes from a framework based in feminine power. Although most of the pieces are written by women, I did not exclude men from this collection. We are all born of women, we are all Gaia's children. The Great Goddess does not belong to women.

The reawakening of feminine deity in the collective unconscious of Western women and men has given birth to a wealth of creative work. May this volume continue to inspire that feminine voice.

BURLEIGH MUTÉN
November 11, 1998

Her Words ✍

INVOCATION

Prayer of Dedication

Cosi Fabian

Inanna, Astarte, Ishtar and Isis,
We reach down the years of women
To Your love and wisdom.

Inanna, Astarte, Ishtar and Isis,
We remember You in the cymbal
And the sweetness of the fig.

Inanna, Astarte, Ishtar and Isis,
We know You by the evening star
And the rhythm of our blood.

Inanna, Astarte, Ishtar and Isis,
We declare You with henna and gold
And the courage of our lives.

Inanna, Astarte, Ishtar and Isis,
We offer You our bodies to love
And speak Your words.

Inanna, Astarte, Ishtar and Isis,
We reach down the years of women
To Your love and wisdom.

Her Eyes a Thousand Times Over
CHANI DiPRIMA

Have you ever noticed how her toes tickle
the water as she runs across
      a fish would drown sooner than she
Full   spirit   lighter   than   air
Have you ever noticed the way she approaches
the sun
      a star is more intimidated by this heat
She is watching us from a certain cloud
hanging from a knowing star
finding rainbows
        rarities.

Is she flesh? Of course, not really.
She'll soar the sky, as wild as any bird
she sees no ground
         enters   deeper   further
     earth so wide
She doesn't look for direction as she is
     approaching   destination
Walk amongst the waters
fly with unseen tree tops
she cries with joy when
the rain of some draining soul saturates the earth
with atmosphere and humid emotion.
She is a glowing smile swallowing
life through her pores   continuing
to dance a hundred dances   traveling this
universe without appreciation   to   anything yet

cherishing all encounters, not one
comparison to ponder, for all originality
        is born in her
she flies with her own and has
fulfillment with absolutely every part of the world.
Emotion is felt by natural wonders so all she
knows is how she feels
The wind whispers to her the truth—silence—
        as she listens her last earthly encounter
is forgotten—the next is all so new.
But the feeling of memory has been remaining
throughout.

Understanding all   it's all an understanding
        She is a simple reflection, flesh   and
not at all you or I.   She might know all
        but she understands even more
willing to be free
and free to be willing.
Options unbounded and real present patience
and truth eternally   continue on and on
        she continues
She is reality   resembling
spirituality   and representing as flesh
not quite so real though   she realizes too many
wonders within to be you or I.
The stars are her eyes a thousand times over.
Have you ever noticed her beauty, so hard to miss
just as easy to take for granted.
        She's unreal
Her beauty and strength not so,
Let her walk on the waters   catch all the fire
        see nothing

but empty reflecting beauty
a roaming soul of the earth.

As she sleeps her dreams show no difference to
her than life   I wonder why
Innocence, youth and complete truth are in her   she
has living emotions
conquered curiosity.
Solidity in tranquil light   stability withstanding in
all that is presented to any emotion.
Complete unawareness to utter consciousness
She need understand nothing for she is
        faithful   to   fate.
She need not be understood for fate is faithful to her.
Have you ever   noticed how her toes tickle the water
        as she walks across the beauty of earth
in this reflection water is solid and the light is glaring
cover your eyes—be blind
Have you ever noticed how she approaches the sun
        her eyes are the stars a thousand times over.

The Second Coming
SUZANNE BENTON

Clouds out of darkness,
Pillow white, they float,
As dawn slides open.
Slowly, the kinswoman
Parachutes gentle free
Arriving with gravity,
Cleaving, to earth,
As Seagull does to nest.

Oracle of all dreams,
Chalice, shelter, wing,
Harvesting molten treasure,
Flowing through sun gold
Feathers and life air of Anatolia.

Ancient fire haired druid, mariner,
Tiamat, Diana, moon world goddess,
Eating the ripe sea, the sensuous air,
Gleaning and swelling the life source
Into a vivid, retina burning, sun flood.
Drenching all completeness with desire
To search sweet for inner seed,
Kindling, bringing to light what is
Herself, the kinswoman.

We Need a God Who Bleeds Now

NTOZAKE SHANGE

we need a god who bleeds now
a god whose wounds are not
some small male vengeance
some pitiful concession to humility
a desert swept with dryin marrow in honor of the lord

we need a god who bleeds
spreads her lunar vulva & showers us in shades of scarlet
thick & warm like the breath of her
our mothers tearing   to let us   in
this place breaks open
like our mothers bleeding
the planet is heaving   mourning our ignorance
the moon tugs the seas
to hold her/ to hold her
embrace swelling hills/ i am
not wounded i am bleeding to life

we need a god who bleeds now
whose wounds are not the end of anything

Grand Grand Mother is returning

JUDY GRAHN

The egg is always being made
and making,
always getting laid
and laying;
thread is being spun
and spinning,
truth is being found
and finding,
getting all unwound
and winding,
being all unsnarled
and snarling,
and the Grand Grand
Mother is returning

that's all I know

Don't suppose it will be
as it is remembered
in time past

time present is a different
unpredicted picture

time future happens
only in the mind

Worlds are always ending
and beginning,
tales are getting learned
and learning,

birds are always taking off
and landing;
the sky is ever being turned
around, and turning;
the tree is ever being stood upon
and standing;
and the flame is getting burned
and burning

Grand Mother is returning
don't expect
the past, expect
whatever happens,
men are moving, more
than ever women are
just wakening;
Grand Grand Mother
is returning

that's all I know

City Goddess

LEAH KORICAN

Goddess of chain link fences
Goddess of street lamps
Goddess of red yellow green
Goddess of black tar

Goddess of help wanted
Goddess of mechanics
Goddess of broken windows
Goddess of public transportation

Goddess of clanking trolley
Goddess of graffiti
Goddess of cracked sidewalk
Goddess of steel suspension span

Goddess of reflective metal
Goddess of reflective glass
Goddess of shining oil spot
Goddess of mirror

Goddess of hard surfaces
walls brick streets curbs
post folding chair
shopping cart

Goddess of smooth surfaces
mirrors painted lines tiles
wood floorboards aluminum

Goddess of soft surfaces
bus seats croissant
french fry silk suit candy bar

Goddess of rectangles
window boxes sidewalk
street truck back open
door newspaper

Goddess of circles
tabletop lamppost eyes
eyes mouth head coffee cup
doughnut eyes eyes quarter
dime stoplight

Goddess of straight lines
money slot sidewalk crack
window molding street line
wait in line rope line
building edge bridge wire

Goddess of wire spark
Goddess of gold
Goddess of glow
Goddess below above
DOWNTOWN
UPTOWN
ALL AROUND GODDESS
Goddess of on time
Goddess of too late
Goddess of wait
wait wait wait
WALK
Goddess of high heels
GODDESS OF TRUCK ROAR
GODDESS OF SIRENS
GODDESS OF EDGES
GODDESS OF ORANGE DIVIDER CONES
GODDESS OF FLOWER STANDS
GODDESS OF CIGARETTE BUTTS

GODDESS OF WASTE PAPER
GODDESS OF WASTE
GODDESS OF PAPER
GODDESS OF WASTE
GODDESS OF GREEN EXIT
GODDESS OF WHITE ENTER
GOING GODDESS
GODDESS RETURNING
GODDESS GOING
RETURNING GODDESS
GODDESS WHO NEVER LEFT

from *Tribute to the Angels*
H.D.

We have seen her
the world over,

Our Lady of the Goldfinch,
Our Lady of the Candelabra,

Our Lady of the Pomegranate,
Our Lady of the Chair;

we have seen her, an empress,
magnificent in pomp and grace,

and we have seen her
with a single flower

or a cluster of garden-pinks
in a glass beside her;

we have seen her snood
drawn over her hair,

or her face set in profile
with the blue hood and stars;

we have seen her head bowed down
with the weight of a domed crown,

or we have seen her, a wisp of a girl
trapped in a golden halo . . .

Radioactive

JANINE CANAN

Chernobyl,
Eniwetok,
Three Mile Island,
Hiroshima,
Jorñada del Muerte,
Nagasaki,
Nevada,
Palomares,
Spokane Reservation—

radioactive forever.
The feminization of everything
is required.

They say she is veiled

JUDY GRAHN

They say she is veiled
and a mystery. That is
one way of looking.
Another
is that she is where
she always has been,
exactly in place,
and it is we,
we who are mystified,
we who are veiled
and without faces.

SALUTATIONS

The Holy Priestess of Heaven

ANONYMOUS

translated by Diane Wolkstein and Samuel Noah Kramer

CA. 2500 BCE

I say, "Hail!" to the Holy One who appears in the heavens!
I say, "Hail!" to the Holy Priestess of Heaven!
I say, "Hail!" to Inanna, Great Lady of Heaven!

Holy Torch! You fill the sky with light!
You brighten the day at dawn!

I say, "Hail!" to Inanna, Great Lady of Heaven!

Awesome Lady of the Annuna Gods! Crowned with great horns,
You fill the heavens and earth with light!

I say, "Hail!" to Inanna, First Daughter of the Moon!

Mighty, majestic, and radiant,
You shine brilliantly in the evening,
You brighten the day at dawn,
You stand in the heavens like the sun and the moon,
Your wonders are known both above and below,
To the greatness of the holy priestess of heaven,
To you, Inanna, I sing!

Litany to Our Lady

ANONYMOUS
translated by Eugene O'Curry

O Great Mary.
O Mary, greatest of Maries.
O Greatest of Women.
O Queen of Angels.
O Mistress of the Heavens.
O Woman full and replete with the grace of the Holy Ghost.
O Blessed and Most Blessed.
O Mother of Eternal Glory.
O Mother of the heavenly and earthly Church.
O Mother of Love and Indulgence.
O Mother of the Golden Heights.
O Honour of the Sky.
O Sign of Tranquility.
O Gate of Heaven.
O Golden Casket.
O Couch of Love and Mercy.
O Temple of Divinity.
O Beauty of Virgins.
O Mistress of the Tribes.
O Fountain of the Parterres.
O Cleansing of the Sins.
O Purifying of Souls.
O Mother of Orphans.
O Breast of the Infants.
O Solace of the Wretched.
O Star of the Sea.
O Handmaid of the Lord.
O Mother of Christ.

O Resort of the Lord.

O Graceful like the Dove.

O Serene like the Moon.

O Resplendent like the Sun.

O Canceling Eve's disgrace.

O Regeneration of Life.

O Beauty of Women.

O Leader of the Virgins.

O Enclosed Garden.

O Closely Locked Fountain.

O Mother of God.

O Perpetual Virgin.

O Holy Virgin.

O Serene Virgin.

O Chaste Virgin.

O Temple of the Living God.

O Royal Throne of the Eternal King.

O Sanctuary of the Holy Ghost.

O Virgin of the Root of Jesse.

O Cedar of Mount Lebanon.

O Cypress of Mount Sion.

O Crimson Rose of the Land of Jacob.

O Blooming like the Palm Tree.

O Fruitful like the Olive Tree.

O Glorious Son-Bearer.

O Light of Nazareth.

O Glory of Jerusalem.

O Beauty of the World.

O Noblest-Born of the Christian Flock.

O Queen of Life.

O Ladder of Heaven.

Hail Mother full of grace power is with thee

JENNIFER BEREZAN

Hail Mother full of grace power is with thee
Blessed are you Queen of the universe and blessed is all of creation
Holy Mother, maker of all things
Be with us now and always Blessed be.

Tantric Praise of the Goddess

ANONYMOUS
adapted by Jalaja Bonheim

Salutations to the goddess who dwells in all things as
the energy of infinite goodness,
salutations again and again.

Salutations to the goddess who dwells in all things as
their innermost nature,
salutations again and again.

Salutations to the goddess who dwells in all things as
the light of consciousness,
salutations again and again.

Salutations to the goddess who dwells in all things as
intelligence, salutations again and again.

Salutations to the goddess who dwells in all things as
sleep, salutations again and again.

Salutations to the goddess who dwells in all things as
hunger, salutations again and again.

Salutations to the goddess who dwells in all things as
desire, salutations again and again.

Salutations to the goddess who dwells in all things as
chaos, salutations again and again.

Salutations to the goddess who dwells in all things as
fierceness, salutations again and again.

Salutations to the goddess who dwells in all things as
change, salutations again and again.

Salutations to the goddess who dwells in all things as beauty, salutations again and again.

Salutations to the goddess who dwells in all things as compassion, salutations again and again.

Salutations to the goddess who dwells in all things as peace, salutations again and again.

The New Our Father

PRISCILLA BAIRD HINCKLEY

Our Mother who art in Earth and Heaven,
(as we are in the MOTHER
and HEAVEN is in us)
Hallowed, respectful, joyful thy name.
Thy holy realm is already come.
Thy will awaits us to be done.
Give us this day the strength to love,
To be the lion and the dove.
Forgive us as we tread your flowers,
Ignoring duties that are ours.
Lead us from annihilation
TO CELEBRATE ALL CREATION,
For we share in the life and in the power
And in the glory forever and ever.

Mother of the Universe

Yoko Ono

Our mother who art of the universe
Hallowed be thy name
Thy wisdom reign, thy will
        is done
As it is to be

You gave us life and protection
And see us through confusion
Teach us love and freedom
As it is to be

For thine is our wisdom and power
Glory forever

For thine is our wisdom and power
Glory forever

Homage to Tara Our Mother

ANONYMOUS

Homage to Tara our mother:
great compassion!
Homage to Tara our mother:
a thousand hands, a thousand eyes!
Homage to Tara our mother:
queen of physicians!
Homage to Tara our mother:
conquering disease like medicine!
Homage to Tara our mother:
knowing the means of compassion!
Homage to Tara our mother:
a foundation like the earth!
Homage to Tara our mother:
cooling like water!
Homage to Tara our mother:
ripening like fire!
Homage to Tara our mother:
spreading like wind!
Homage to Tara our mother:
pervading like space!

The 23rd Psalm

BOBBY MCFERRIN

The Lord is my Shepherd, I have all I need,
She makes me lie down in green meadows,
Beside the still waters, She will lead.

She restores my soul, She rights my wrongs,
She leads me in a path of good things,
And fills my heart with songs.

Even though I walk through a dark and dreary land,
There is nothing that can shake me,
She has said she won't forsake me,
I'm in her hand.

She sets a table before me in the presence of my foes,
She anoints my head with oil,
And my cup overflows.

Surely, surely goodness and kindness will follow me
All the days of my life,
And I will live in her house
Forever, forever and ever.

Glory be to our Mother, and Daughter,
And to the Holy of Holies,
As it was in the beginning, is now and ever shall be,
World, without end. Amen.

The Song

ANNE BARING

Beehive source
Trellised womb
Mother of all beginnings

Hold me
Gather me
Feed me
With the honey-nectar
From the hive.

Nourished
I will sing
The Bee-song
The long-forgotten threnody
Of praise to thee.

A Pledge of Allegiance to the Family of Earth

MIM KELBER

I pledge allegiance to the Earth,
and to the flora, fauna
and human life that it supports,
one planet, indivisible,
with safe air, water and soil,
economic justice, equal rights
and peace for all.

THE GROUND
OF OUR BEING

The Valley Spirit never dies

LAO-TZU
translated by Arthur Waley

The Valley Spirit never dies,
It is named the Mysterious Female.
And the doorway of the Mysterious Female
Is the base from which Heaven and Earth sprang.
It is there within us all the while.
Draw upon it as you will, it never runs dry.

The Hymn to the Earth

HOMER
translated by Charles Boer

The mother of us all,
the oldest of all,
hard,
    splendid as rock

Whatever there is that is of the land
        it is she
            who nourishes it,
       it is the Earth
           that I sing

Whoever you are,
howsoever you come
       across her sacred ground
    you of the sea,
    you that fly,
it is she
   who nourishes you
  she,
     out of her treasures
          Beautiful children
          beautiful harvests
            are achieved from you
          The giving of life itself,
          the taking of it back
          to or from
            any man
              are yours

The happy man is simply
                        the man you favor
the man who has your favor
                        and that man
                                    has everything
            His soil thickens
            it becomes heavy with life,
            his cattle grow fat in their fields,
            his house fills up with things

These are the men who govern a city with good laws
                and the women of their city,
                the women are beautiful
                                fortune
                                wealth,
                                            it all follows

            Their sons glory
                        in the ecstasy of youth
            Their daughters play,
                        they dance in the flowers,
                                they skip
                                            in and out
                        on the grass
                                    over soft flowers

It is you
        the goddess
it is you who honored them

Now,
mother of gods,
                bride of the sky
                            in stars
        farewell:

but if you liked what I sang here
give me this life too
                    then,
                    in my other poems
                                        I will remember you

The earth is at the same time mother

HILDEGARD OF BINGEN
translated by Gabriele Uhlein

The earth is at the same time
mother,
she is mother of all that is natural,
    mother of all that is human.
She is the mother of all,
for contained in her
are the seeds of all.

Epiphany

PEM KREMER

Lynn Schmidt says
    she saw You once as prairie grass,
    Nebraska prairie grass,

    she climbed out of her car on a hot highway
    leaned her butt on the nose of her car,
    looked out over one great flowing field,
    stretching beyond her sight until the horizon came:
    vastness, she says,
    responsive to the *slightest shift* of wind,
        full of infinite change,
        all One.

She says when she can't pray
She calls up Prairie Grass.

God's Body

SARA KLUGMAN

This tree is God's challah,
when you cut it
the Hebrew letters fly out.
All the people are all cells.
All the trees in the world
are God's body,
the animals are God's feet
and the whole world is walking.
All the animals' hands
are God's hands.
The mountains are God's knees.
The snow is God's tears.
Our smiles are God's eyebrows.
The mud is God's blood.
The long branches are God's arms,
the flowers are Her sense of smell and Her ears.
The grass is God's hair.
God's songs are birds.
Our words are God's voice.

He Na Tye Woman

Paula Gunn Allen

Water.
Lakes and rivers.
Oceans and streams.
Springs, pools and gullies.
Arroyos, creeks, watersheds.
Pacific. Atlantic. Mediterranean.
Indian. Caribbean. China Sea.
(Lying. Dreaming on shallow shores.)
Arctic. Antarctic. Baltic.
Mississippi. Amazon. Columbia. Nile.
Thames. Sacramento. Snake. (undulant woman river.)
Seine. Rio Grande. Willamette. McKenzie. Ohio.
Hudson. Po. Rhine. Rhone.
Rain. After a lifetime of drought.
That finally cleanses the air.
The soot from our eyes.
The dingy windows of our western home.
The rooftops and branches. The wings of birds.
The new light on a slant. Pouring. Making everything new.

Water (woman) that is the essence of you.
He na tye (woman) that is recognition and remembering.
Gentle. Soft. Sure.
Long shadows of afternoon, growing as the light turns
west toward sleep. Turning with the sun.
(The rest of it is continents and millennia.
(How could I have waited so long for completion?)

The water rises around us like the goddess coming home.
(Arisen.) Same trip, all things considered, all times

and visions, all places and spaces taken into account
on that ancient journey, finally returned. The maps, the plans,
the timetables: the carefully guided tours into all manner
of futilities. Manners the last turn in the road: arid irony.

(Lady, why does your love touch me?
(Lady, why do my hands have strength for you?
(Lady, how could I wander so long without you?

Water in Falls, misting and booming on the rocks below.
Tall pines in the mist, the deep carved caves.
Water in rivulets. Gathering speed, drops joining in headlong
    flight.
Unnamed rivers, flowing eternally underground, unchanging,
    unchanged.
Water thundering down long dry arroyos, the ancient causeways
of our faith. Drought over, at last. Carrying silt,
bits of broken glass, branches, pebbles, pieces of abandoned cars,
parts of lost houses and discarded dreams. Downstream.
Storms of water, and we
deluged
singing
hair plastered to our ecstatic skulls,
waving wild fists at the bolts hurled at us from above
teeth shimmering in the sheets of rain (the sheen)
eyes blinded with the torrents that fall fromthroughover them:
Rain. The Rain that makes us new.
The rain is you.
How did I wait so long to drink.

I am the one whose praise

HILDEGARD OF BINGEN
translated by Gabriele Uhlein

I am the one whose praise
echoes on high.
I adorn all the earth.
I am the breeze
that nurtures all things
green.
I encourage blossoms to flourish with ripening fruits.
I am led by the spirit to feed
the purest streams.
I am the rain
coming from the dew
that causes the grasses to laugh
with the joy of life.
I call forth tears,
the aroma of holy work.
I am the yearning for good.

The Planet Earth Speaks

Alma Luz Villanueva

1

I spin through time
and darkness: I glue

you to me with love.
I house your body

with earth, your
soul with air.

You swim toward
me each night crying,

"Mother." You have not
forgotten me: I am

too vast; my heart
too hot; my blood
too sweet; my beauty
too astounding. I

reveal this to you
because it is not
a secret, or is
it hidden from

your view. I am
entirely obvious:

I am spinning through
the fabric of your
dreams. I am ever

present. I am an
ancient pattern within
you, without you,

and you've never escaped
my scrutiny or
my stare. You are
glued to me, but, yes,

I've also taught you
flight. I am flying
through the present
time, forever. I am

the maker of wonders,
the maker of horrors,
the maker of beauty,
the maker of terror:

and I made you to
love me whole, small
echo of my womb:
to love me as I

love you.
Unconditionally.

2

The pattern of butterfly
wings, eagle's back,
hawk feather, fox
ear, coyote tail,
whale fin, dolphin
belly, eel eye,
tree trunk, human
hand, veined leaf,

the heart, dividing
crystal, stone's basin,
the lips, peach skin,
peach flesh, the teeth,
wet pit, white blossom,
fragrance-in-the-air,
cellular structure, two
eyes, all wombs,
red-head-of-the-hummingbird,
dragonfly glitter, moth
down, reptile flesh,
deep mud, each snowflake,
all scrotums, sweet
flowers, such cactus,
the hair, newborn things,
sacred fire, sacred water,
much fur, many vegetables,
baby feet, one tomato, I

give you
Unconditionally.

3

The stars keep watch,
my sisters; my mother
the moon, my lover
the sun, my daughters
the galaxy and sons
of my space; my father
who journeyed to the
moon, my beautiful
mother he would die
for and has only to

kiss her heart more
clearly with his own
spark-of-the-sun:
they listen for songs
of praise, the ancient
words
of love, of worship:
they see a destruction
growing in my belly:
they hear the words
of hate, and they
feel the loneliness
of those who are
born and die
without loving.
Unconditionally.

4

I am spinning, twirling
in my dance that
draws you close to
me. There is no

silence, only pause.
There is no stillness,
only pause. There
is sound, an endless

spiral. There is movement,
an endless spiral. There
is no death, but pause.
There is life, this spiral.

I am but the dust on the
edge of what shimmers in
the telling wind that tells
me, *you know everything.*

> *To Ayla, which means wing—*
> *a newborn girlchild born April 1983.*

From the Healing Dark

ALMA LUZ VILLANUEVA

She is rising. Yes,
she is rising. My

Earth is rising.

Beware of an angry woman,
life is hers to give and take.

Everything has its limits, even
love, though what goes on is

love,

and what survives belongs to
the light. And she is rising.

She is rising to the light:
moon and sun, grandmother and mother

to her soul, her heart.
She will not tolerate fools

or lies any longer.

To Leah Tutu, slinging mud at a
tour bus in Soweto, South Africa

The Search

INGE HOOGERHUIS

Go underneath the ancient moss
Where the smell of earth and
Woman is.

Push through small, heavy boulders
And sand chafing hands
Until you hit clay, red-brown,
The color of a heart still pumping.

Go further,
Forget you are digging in my chest.
Bending my sternum aside.

Blind, deaf, and dumb
I sense a presence
But my flailing arms
Only knock candles over,
Scorching my palms.

I need help
To weave my fingers through my lungs
To where deer lay down to foal,
Where children shout
Allee Allee Axun Free,
Where muffled cries form words
And sperm and egg
Meet, in glorious innocence.

the earth is a living thing

LUCILLE CLIFTON

is a black shambling bear
ruffling its wild back and tossing
mountains into the sea

is a black hawk circling
the burying ground circling the bones
picked clean and discarded

is a fish black blind in the belly of water
is a diamond blind in the black belly of coal

is a black and living thing
is a favorite child
of the universe
feel her rolling her hand
in its kinky hair
feel her brushing it clean

Our Mother

SUSAN GRIFFIN

At the center of the earth there is a mother.
If any of us who are her children choose to die
she feels a grief like a wound deeper
than any of us can imagine.
She puts her hands to her face
like this: her palms open.
Put them there as she does.
Her fingers press into her eyes.
Do that, too.
She tries to howl.
Some of us have decided
this mother cannot hear all of us
in our desperate wishes.
Here, in this time,
our hearts have been cut into small chambers
like ration cards
and we can no longer imagine every
morsel nor each tiny
thought at once,
as *she* still can.
This is normal,
she tries to tell us,
but we don't listen.
Sometimes someone has a faint memory
of all this, and
she suffers.
She is wrong to imagine
she suffers alone.
Do you think we are not all hearing and speaking

at the same time?
Our mother is somber.
She is thinking.
She puts her big ear
against the sky
to comfort herself.
Do this. She calls to us,
Do this.

The fields belong to woman
BETTY DE SHONG MEADOR

The fields belong to woman. In her body, woman carries the secret knowledge of fertility and growing. Woman is like the field. The field and the woman both caress the seed. The seed is at home in her body and in the earth's body. The seed feeds off the moist nurturing food her blood carries and the earth carries. Her body naturally harbors the seed in her womb. The seed grows. The mystery astounds her. And she is the mystery. Wisely, the fields belong to woman.

from *Medea speaks*

Z BUDAPEST

Medea speaks:
This is God, children, listen up well. The
beautiful blue planet, our mother, our sister.
She moves with 200 miles per second, yet
imperceptible; she offers the quiet of the lakes
and the rushing of her rivers, the vast expanse
of her oceans, the echoes of her mountains.
This is God, children . . . listen up well.
Lift your eyes to the heavens, and you behold
her sisters the stars and her cousins the suns
and nebulas, and fill your senses with her
infinite beauty. . . .

Yemoja

Baba Ifa Karade

Yemoja, mother of the fishes,
Mother of the waters on the earth.
Nurture me, my mother
Protect and guide me.
Like the waves of the ocean,
Wash away the trials that I bear.
Grant me children.
Grant me peace.
Let not the witches devour me.
Let not evil people destroy me.
Yemoja, mother of all,
Nurture me my mother.

When She Laughs

JUDITH SORNBERGER

It's the boom of ice
cracking across lakes,
waking you from deepest dream
as it wakes the water,
lighting a match
in the memory of fish.

Its wake sends ripples
to our toes and fingertips.
We itch to dance *en pointe*.
We want to dig, eclipse
with earth the moons
rising from our cuticles.

(Bread rises.
Kindling catches.
Seeds burst their cases.
Ideas fall open like tulips.
For a moment we all
want to live forever.)

It hangs forever in the air—
a neon mist, catalogued as the Owl
Nebula, the Ring. New stars blink on
blue-white in the Pleiades,
the Universe Her library of laughter.

It's the deep-won laugh of an old woman.
Black-winged, raucous, diving
circles, swirling the air
with its antics.

Laugh deep in the body,
laugh down to your soul.
She considers it an invocation,
swoops in the open window,
lets you near Her.

The Charge of the Goddess

DOREEN VALIENTE
adapted by Starhawk

I who am the beauty of the green earth and the white moon among the stars and the mysteries of the waters, I call upon your soul to arise and come unto me. For I am the soul of nature that gives life to the universe. From Me all things proceed and unto Me they must return. Let My worship be in the heart that rejoices, for behold—all acts of love and pleasure are My rituals. Let there be beauty and strength, power and compassion, honor and humility, mirth and reverence within you. And you who seek to know Me, know that your seeking and yearning will avail you not, unless you know the Mystery: for if that which you seek, you find not within yourself, you will never find it without. For behold, I have been with you from the beginning, and I am that which is attained at the end of desire.

Holy Goddess Tellus

ANONYMOUS
SECOND CENTURY CE

Holy Goddess Tellus,
Mother of Living Nature,
The food of life
Thou metest out in eternal loyalty
And, when life has left us,
We take our refuge in Thee.
Thus everything Thou dolest out
Returns into Thy womb.
Rightly Thou art called Mother of the Gods.
Because by Thy loyalty
Thou hast conquered the power of the Gods.
Verily Thou art also the Mother
Of the peoples and the Gods,
Without Thee nothing can thrive nor be;
Thou art powerful, of the Gods Thou art
The Queen and also the Goddess.
Thee, Goddess, and Thy power I now invoke;
Thou canst easily grant all that I ask,
And in exchange I will give Thee, Goddess, sincere thanks.

THE ANCIENTS CALL

Re-member Us

JUDITH ANDERSON

Re-member us,
you who are living,
restore us, renew us.
Speak for our silence.
Continue our work.
Bless the breath of life.
Sing of the hidden patterns.
Weave the web of peace.

Cicada

ECLIPSE

Ancient One, Wise One, Old Mother,
aged woman squatting in the sand,
like a primordial bird
hovering and waiting in the stillness.
The only movement is your feathers shifting
with the dry wind.
Warm sand bulges into form,
outlining copper tones on blue skies.
The heat is healing your bones as it dries your skin.
Out of the desert's silence I hear the panting of your
hot breath, pulsating across time.
And then I hear many hot breaths.
I see many squatting women in a circle.
The Ancient Ones
breathing life into Earth's body.

And the cicada tells me it is time.

The Ancient Ones, whose glance carries the power
of a hawk's claw.
The Ancient Ones, whose eyes search mine,
bringing me back.
The Ancient Ones, whose hands reach out
touching my deep longing.

Aged Ones, Old Ones, Wise Mothers,
across time I whisper for you to come.
My laments turn into rhythmic moans,
moving deep within me.

And the cicada tells me it is time.

Across all boundaries and time, I return to you,
Goddesses of our ways.
I taste your sweet fruit warmed by the sun,
soothing my dried throat.
I call to you
uncoiling like the serpent,
rhythms open, stirring inside me.
My deep throated call beckons across the desert
answered by squatting women in open spaces.

And the cicada tells us it is time.

The serpent spirals outward across sound.
Our voice becomes her voice,
her vibrations ripple through us,
turning time into rhythm and rhythm into time.

Spinning, I find myself between the Ancient and the Aged.
Oh, Ancient Mother, Aged One, can you see me as I see you?

Old Woman, your temple lies still in your heart,
but all dear to you lives in me.

And for this moment we will forget the pain,
the stones crumbling from our temples,
the fires burning our bodies,
the raged wars and then the silence.

For this moment we will remember the fire
as our sacred flame in the wells of the temples.
We will remember the dark blue and white mosaic
patterns that swirled as we danced.
We will remember the women hand in hand, moving to the
blue flame that emerged from the darkness of the earth.

And the cicada tells us it is time.

For this moment our serpents uncoil together.
Deep into my spiral I weave into yours,

and within the beat, my body sways, touching yours.
Old One, Wise One,
our palms press
our hearts breathe
our spirits dance our power, knowing the sacred flame
lives.
It is ours inside forever!
Together, we dance the return.
We shapeshift our place, our time.
For one moment across the sands
I become you and you become me
  The Old Ones
  The Wise Ones
  The Ancient Ones.

The Ancient Ones

PATRICIA REIS

From the beginning,
We have been with you.
We are the ancient ones
And we remember.

We remember the time when there was only love,
The time when all breathing was one.
We remember the seed of your being
Planted in the belly of the vast black night.
We remember the red cave of deep slumber,
The time of forgetting,
The sound of your breath,
The pulse of your heart.
We remember the force
Of your longing for life,
The cries of your birth
Bringing you forth.
We are the ancient ones
And we have waited
                    and watched.

You say that you cannot remember that time
That you have no memory of us.
You say that you cannot hear our voices
That our touch no longer moves you.
You say there can be no return
That something has been lost,
That there is only
                    silence.

We say the time of waiting is over.
We say the silence has been broken.
We say there can be no forgetting now.
We say
                listen

We are the bones of your grandmother's grandmothers.
We have returned now
We say you cannot forget us now
We say we are with you
And you are us.
Remember
                Remember.

She Who Listens

ELANA KLUGMAN

Shma—listen, receive
what has been broken,
longs to return, open
the dark cramped places, let
walls crumble, let pain lift,
all the tired, overused burdens.

Shshshsh—ma
the necessary quiet, letting
go of sound and self, cleansing
into speech.

Sh Ma Ma—She who brings
us through Mitzrayim, the narrow
straits, who holds us to Her breast, knows
us as seed and branch.

Sh shemesh—sun, light arranging
sky and cloud, the indrawing,
indwelling nectar,
what calls us awake.

Shma—She who sits
us on Her great hip, who we bring
stones, all the storied
days of our lives, who hears
my voice when I remember
to speak.

NOTE: *Shma* is the first word and name for one of the most central prayers in Jewish liturgy. The word *shma* in Hebrew means "listen." *Mitzrayim* is the Hebrew word for "the narrow straits" and is also the biblical word for *Egypt*. The word *shemesh* means "sun."

EARTH'S
DAUGHTERS

INANNA 🖎

Lady of Largest Heart

ENHEDUANNA
translated by Betty De Shong Meador

Your torch flames
heaven's four quarters
spreads splendorous light in the dark
you have realized
the Queen of Heaven and Earth
to the utmost
you hold everything
entirely in your hands
your storm-shot torrents drench the bare earth
moisten to life
moisture bearing light
floods the dark
O my Lady, my queen
I unfold your splendor in all lands
I extol your glory
I will praise your course
your sweeping grandeur forever.
Queen, Mistress
you are sublime
you are venerable
your great deeds
are boundless
may I praise
your eminence
O maiden Inanna
sweet is your praise

The Lady Who Ascends into the Heavens

ANONYMOUS

translated by Diane Wolkstein and Samuel Noah Kramer

CA. 2500 BCE

My Lady, the Amazement of the Land, the Lone Star,
The Brave One who appears first in the heavens—
All the lands fear her.

In the pure places of the steppe,
On the high roofs of the dwellings,
On the platforms of the city,
They make offerings to her:
Piles of incense like sweet-smelling cedar,
Fine sheep, fat sheep, long-haired sheep,
Butter, cheese, dates, fruits of all kinds.

They purify the earth for My Lady.
They celebrate her in song.
They fill the table of the land with the first fruits.
They pour dark beer for her.
They pour light beer for her.
Dark beer, emmer beer,
Emmer beer for My Lady.

The *sagub*-vat and the *lamsari*-vat make a bubbling noise for her.
They prepare *gug*-bread in date syrup for her.
Flour, flour in honey, beer at dawn.
They pour wine and honey for her at sunrise.

The gods and the people of Sumer go to her with food and drink.
They feed Inanna in the pure clean place.

My Lady looks in sweet wonder from heaven.
The people of Sumer parade before the holy Inanna.
Inanna, the Lady Who Ascends into the Heavens, is radiant.
I sing your praises, holy Inanna.
The Lady Who Ascends into the Heavens is radiant on the horizon.

Inanna's Chant

Janine Canan

Heaven is Hers!
Earth is Hers!
She is a warrior,
She is a falcon,
She is a great white cow.
She fought the dragon and slew it.
She seduced the scorpion and tamed it.
The golden lion sleeps at Her side.
She is the singer,
She is desire.
She is the mountain of silver, gold and lapis.
On Her hips tall trees grow, and grasses.
From Her waters spout, and savory grains.
Her lap is holy,
Her lips are honey,
Her hand is law.
Her breast pours heavenly rain.
She is the healer,
She is life-giver,
She is the terror, the anger, the hunger.
Fierce winds blow from Her heart.
Hers is the thunder, the lightning, the glory.
She is the morning,
She is the evening,
She is the star.
She wears the gown of mystery.
Heaven is Hers!
Earth is Hers!
Who can argue?

The Lady of the Morning

ANONYMOUS

translated by Diane Wolkstein and Samuel Noah Kramer
CA. 2500 BCE

Honored Counselor, Ornament of Heaven, Joy of An!
When sweet sleep has ended in the bedchamber,
You appear like bright daylight.

When all the lands and the people of Sumer assemble,
Those sleeping on the roofs and those sleeping by the walls,
When they sing your praises, bringing their concerns to you,
You study their words.

You render a cruel judgment against the evildoer;
You destroy the wicked.
You look with kindly eyes on the straightforward;
You give that one your blessing.

My Lady looks in sweet wonder from heaven.
The people of Sumer parade before the holy Inanna.
Inanna, the Lady of the Morning, is radiant.
I sing your praises, holy Inanna.
The Lady of the Morning is radiant on the horizon.

Choice
Inanna and the Galla
PEM KREMER

Helpless on a meathook
she hangs naked:

the circle of her belly reflects the Sun Above;
her necklace droops below her belly button;

down-drawing
elongates her fingers
melts her feet into the pit;

the galla gloat and drool into the Great Below:

her eyes open.

from *Loud Thundering Storm*

Anonymous

translated by Diane Wolkstein and Samuel Noah Kramer

CA. 2500 BCE

Proud Queen of the Earth Gods, Supreme Among the Heaven
    Gods,
Loud Thundering Storm, you pour your rain over all the lands
    and all the people.
You make the heavens tremble and the earth quake.
Great Priestess, who can soothe your troubled heart?

You flash like lightning over the highlands; you throw your
    firebrands across the earth.
Your deafening command, whistling like the South Wind, splits
    apart great mountains.
You trample the disobedient like a wild bull; heaven and earth
    tremble.
Holy Priestess, who can soothe your troubled heart?

Your frightful cry descending from the heavens devours
    its victims.
Your quivering hand causes the midday heat to hover over
    the sea.
Your nighttime stalking of the heavens chills the land with its
    dark breeze.

Holy Inanna, the riverbanks overflow with the flood-waves
    of your heart. . . .

ISIS

May Isis heal me

ANONYMOUS

May Isis heal me as she healed her son Horus.
O Isis! Thou great enchantress, heal me, save me
from all evil things of darkness, from the epidemic
and deadly diseases and infections of all sorts that
spring upon me, as thou hast saved and freed thy son Horus,
for I have passed through fire and am come out of the water. . . .
Free me from all possible evil, hurtful things of darkness,
from epidemic and deadly fevers of all kinds.

I who am Nature, mother of all

LUCIUS APULEIUS

I, who am Nature, the mother of all things, the mistress of all the
elements, the primordial offspring of time, the supreme among
Divinities, the queen of departed spirits, the first of the celestials,
and the uniform manifestation of the Gods and Goddesses; who
govern by my nod the luminous heights of heaven, the salubrious
breezes of the ocean, and the anguished silent realms of the shades
below: whose one sole divinity the whole orb of the earth
venerates under a manifold form, with different rites, and under a
variety of appellations. Hence the Phyrygians, that primaeval race,
call me Pessinuntica, the Mother of the Gods; the Aborigines of
Attica, Cecropian Minerva; the Cyprians, in their sea-girt isle,
Paphian Venus; the arrow-bearing Cretans, Diana Dictynna; the
three-tongued Sicilians, Stygian Proserpine; and the Eleusinians,
the ancient Goddess Ceres. Some call me Juno, others, Bellona,
others Hecate, and others Rhamnusia. But those who are
illumined by the earliest rays of that divinity, the Sun, when he
rises, the Ethiopians, the Arii, and the Egyptians, so skilled in
ancient learning, worshiping me with ceremonies quite
appropriate, call me by my true name, Queen Isis. Behold then,
. . . I come to thy assistance; favouring and propitious I am come.

Isis (Lady of Petals)

JONATHAN COTT

1

Lady of Petals,
gone into Underworld
trying to find the perfect flower—
white or yellow, with streaks
of pink in candlelight—
softer than the linen on your golden body,
adorned with every star of heaven—
mirror on your forehead
serpents by your side—whatever you are called—
Diana . . . Demeter,
Ishtar . . . Isis—
one breathes your perfumed air
through nights of sweetest sleep
until your mirror becomes the sun,
and I wake up—
like a face lost in the light,
like a voice lost in the wind,
like a heart lost in flowers.

2

This scent—
purer than the odor of your neck,
stronger than the sound of the letters of your name

Inhaling deeply,
holding my breath,
I turn myself into the inside and the outside of your being

This scent dissolving me

3

By the terrace light
Through the blinds
Of the hotel room
I watch your eyes
Closed all night long
And in the shadows
Listen to the wind
Listen to the trees
Listen to the sea

4

On a hot night
you bring me here,
to the edge of the sea,
and point to a ghostly aura
(the lights of Tangier across the waters)

Years ago,
across the waters,
I sat with friends at the outdoor Café Arabe
smoking kif in pipes,
drinking mint tea with orange blossoms,
and looking across the waters
toward us in the future

You were only seven years old then,
with dark, wide-open eyes—

staring straight ahead—
and now you leave me here,
alone in this world,
with the trees going mad in the wind.

5

Whenever you leave
I can't remember
what you look like
anymore

(Only your scent
in the palms of my hands)

6

They say that God is a bud of jasmine
planted in the heart.
Every night I used to feel it,
coming up from the roots.
I would stand very still in the dark,
my arms outstretched,
waiting in the air . . .
until one night,
from nowhere,
a breeze of kindness startled me,
I started moving
(just a little)—
branches trembling,
petals falling,
scent rising—
and then I closed my eyes,
I let my fragrance take me anywhere,
I heard my heart beat everywhere

7

Every night,
in humidity and heat,
a breeze sends the smell of jasmine
across the southern tourist towns,
till everything is still,
everyone insensible—
a realm of opiated sighs—
except for those who hold
white and yellow petals
(with streaks of pink by moonlight)
in the palms of their hands
and calmly walk the empty, darkened streets—
holding hands in silence
until each petal falls or scatters in a breeze . . .
as one blows off into the hills—
above the shouts and noise returning to the town—
where one bell-ringing, tired donkey
notices a shining petal lodged inside some roots,
works it with his teeth,
chews it patiently,
takes a breath,
inhales its fragrance . . .
then looks up past his blinders
and watches night's sky opening into light
and sees, inside, She Who Makes the Universe Spin Round . . .
Mistress of the Living . . . Mistress of the Dead . . .
Lady of Breath and Splendor . . . Lady of the Deep—
mirror on her forehead,
serpents by her side:
and She is always smiling,
unending jasmine petals falling from her hair.

LILITH ⚡

Liturgy for Lilith
COSI FABIAN

I am Lilith, grandmother of Mary Magdalene.
I am Lilith, whose sexual fire was too hot for God.
I am Lilith, the first woman who chose the rage of exile over
the cancer of servitude.

I am Lilith, mother to the mother-less.
I am Lilith, whose blood covers the moon.
I am Lilith, standing on owl's claws at a woman's crossroads.

I am Lilith, the whore in the gateway of the temple.
I am Lilith, whose serpentine tongue caused Eve to laugh—and
pick the apple!
I am Lilith, revolving sword of flame, scorching hypocrisy from
truth's white bones.

I am Lilith, free-moving in the wilderness.
I am Lilith, spirit of night and air.
I am Lilith, in whose dark caves transgressors find sanctuary.

I am Salome.
I am Morgan Le Faye.
I am the Queen of Shayba
(My hair is black and I am "dark but comely")
Solomon sang my song!
My hair is red and my skin ivory.
I am Eve's big sister.

I am Lilith, mother to the mother-less.
I am Lilith, whose sexual fire was too hot for God.
I am Lilith, living in the shadow—
Waiting—for you.

Lilith

SUZANNE BENTON

I wake in the morning
Thinking I am Lilith
Living by the Red Sea.

That Babylonian Goddess
Born of the dust of the earth
Same as Adam.

That undying first wife,
Leaving Eden
Rather than be subservient,
Crossing the desert to the sea,
Loving daemons and satyrs,
Whoever they might be.

It was cramped in the garden,
A life of repetitious humid languor.
The path to the sea was endless,
The dry burning earth,
Boiling heat suspended in the air.

I lost many children.
The angels hounded me.
Was it God's malice
For leaving his Adam?

It's spring by the sea now.
There's laughter here.
People come in great ships
Singing.
The sun purls on the cool water
Creating kaleidoscopic blues.

My voice is clear in the open space.
There's gaiety, and parades and feasts.
Is this the world of daemons and satyrs?
It's true.
Nothing is as imagined.

The angels hounded her.
Adam was unbending.
She never ate the apple.
She never died.

Lilith and the Doctor

KATHLEEN NORRIS

He shuffled my file,
my life. I had lost the language of
trees in wind,
the river talking to stones.

He wrote in his notebooks:
how a chasm opened
in the ground at my feet,
how I almost drowned
in a whirlpool
that was just a bowl of dough.

And on a sunny afternoon
I'll never forget
the flowers seemed so brittle with cold
I knew they'd break
if I breathed on them.

"You're not constipated?" he asked.
"Do you have trouble getting to sleep?"
"No," I said, "I want to sleep all the time."
"Well, you don't have the clinical signs of depression," he said,
clicking his pen.

I left then, for good,
and as I walked
the song broke through,
the loud green sound
of this garden called the earth,
the garden between my thighs.
The sky's spinning song

of light and dark:
a rocking in my blood,
the ocean's lowing like a cow
looking for her calf.

I sat and sang by the water's edge
where I knew he would not go.

Medusa and Perseus III: Lilith

PAT PARNELL

> *"You can have me if you can catch me." She
> came to me like an angel from heaven. . . . This
> beautiful naked girl's body, pretty blond diamond
> shapes all over her. A rattlesnake head, and her
> tongue was just like a rattlesnake's too, sticking
> out at me.*
> —JESCO WHITE, "The Dancing Outlaw"

Lilith is our daughter,
child of our one-time coupling, hero
and snake goddess joining in frenzy.

Our passion and anger
are mixed in her. She was a handful,
growing up. Wild, mischievous, changeable—
neither her father nor I could manage her.
She follows no law but her own.

She was Adam's first wife.
Motherlike, I warned her it wouldn't work.
I knew Yahweh,
him and his pretty little garden
and all his rules and regulations.

But she wanted the new-formed man,
innocent, unaware, someone she
could shape, make her mate.
But even new-formed, he was still
a man. Wanted his woman subservient.

She is her father's daughter, proud,
hot-headed, subservient to no one.

She escaped to the Red Sea, her
red hair a comet's tail behind her. Yahweh
sent his angels after her, but she was bold.
She pronounced the unpronounceable name
and the angels fled in terror.

Some say she was the serpent who tempted Eve,
making trouble for the second wife.
In the Sistine Chapel, Michelangelo
painted the serpent with breasts
and a woman's face and hair.
I asked her one day, and she laughed.

But after Eden she came to Eve
when Adam was in the fields. Showed her—the
poor innocent—the wifely arts. Cooking, sewing,
spinning and weaving, preserving food.
Birthing, nurturing.
"Someone had to help her out," she told me.
Not the arts of the bed, though. "She won't
need them with him," she said, and laughed.

She visited Solomon as Queen of Sheba,
testing him with her wisdom, teasing him with riddles.
He sang of his love for her, the Dark Goddess,
and she bore his son. I was a grandmother,
tying a red thread on the baby's cradle.

The storytellers called her Demon
for daring to challenge the king.
They loaded all their fears on her, the scapegoat.
Beware of Lilith, the storytellers say:
She hides behind your mirrors, watching you.
All mirrors, they say, are Lilith's gateway
to her caves beneath the sea.

Throughout the years, she has been
viewed with dread—and fascination.

Eternal Temptress, incubus and succubus,
Satan's Bride, mother of demons,
Kayn aynhoreh, the Evil Eye.
She was blamed for witches, those poor women.
And she and I were helpless, watching, able only
to ease their suffering as they burned to death.

I am proud to be her mother.
We are her parents, but she transcends us,
the Uroboric serpent,
joining humanity and divinity.
Queen of the South,
She will arise in Judgment on the Last Day.

She combines the wisdom of the body,
the wisdom of the mind, the wisdom
of the spirit, a sacred trinity. Through dreams
she teaches the joy of complete union, the
promise Adam wouldn't give her.

But woe to those who violate her vision,
demean love, deny it, take it by force.
she leaves them with perpetual priapism,
Adam-like, always unsatisfied,
while she returns, laughing,
triumphant, to her castle on the Red Sea,
leaving her star-shaped footprints on the shore.

ISHTAR ✒

Hymn to Ishtar

ASHUR-NASIR-PAL, KING OF ASSYRIA
CA. 1000 BCE

Unto the queen of the gods, into whose hands are committed the behests of the great gods, unto the Lady of Nineveh, the queen of the gods, the exalted one, unto the daughter of the Moon-god, the twin-sister of the Sun-god, unto her who ruleth all kingdoms, unto the Goddess of the world who determineth decrees, unto the Lady of heaven and earth who receiveth supplication, unto the merciful Goddess who hearkeneth unto entreaty, who receiveth prayer, who loveth righteousness, I make my prayer unto Ishtar, to whom all confusion is a cause of grief. The sorrows which I see I lament before thee. Incline thy ear unto my words of lamentation and let thine heart be opened unto my sorrowful speech. Turn thy face unto me, O Lady, so that be reason thereof the heart of thy servant may be made strong! I, Ashur-nasir-pal, the sorrowful one, am thine humble servant. I, who am beloved by thee, make offerings unto thee and adore thy divinity. . . . I was born in the mountans which no man knoweth; I was without understanding and I prayed not to thy majesty. Moreover, the people of Assyria did not recognize and did not accept thy divinity. But thou, O Ishtar, thou mighty Queen of the gods, by the lifting up of thine eyes didst teach me, for thou didst desire my rule. Thou didst take me from the mountains, and didst make me the Door of the Peoples . . . and thou, O Ishtar, didst make great my name! . . . As concerning that for which thou art wroth with me, grant me forgiveness. Let thine anger be appeased, and let thine heart be mercifully inclined towards me.

Qadesha (Sacred Whore)

COSI FABIAN

The blood of Ishtar,
Goddess of Desire,
Flows through my body.

Isis forms my heart,
Her honey sweetens my vulva.

Astarte moves my womb—
Wanting the hard phallus.
As the Tree of Life seeks the sky,
So my silken limbs entwine the tall king.

My lips are sweet. Life is in my mouth.
Beneath my robes—I am Glorious.

When I dance, the sun sails safely through the night.
When I dance, the future is formed by my feet.
When I dance, the stars move through the heavens.

When I dance, women perfume their thighs, drape gold upon
    their breasts.
When I dance, the maiden laughs and tosses her hair.
When I dance, the youth writes poetry, waits under the moon.
When I dance, the matron teases her husband—the
                husband becomes generous.

When I dance, Venus shimmers the desert.
When I dance, dust becomes silver, stones are made of gold.

SHEKINAH 🦋

Greeting Shekinah

LYNN GOTTLIEB

Two figures face each other,
Sitting close to the earth in the old way;
Outside in the early morn
The women face each other,
Eye to eye, smile to smile,
Squatting over the earth,
Backs curved like earthen pots.
So gracefully they sit,
Pouring water over each other's hands.
Fire pales as the sun rises;
The spice of dew consecrates the hour.
"Shekinah of the sun, Shekinah of the moon,
We greet You with our morning song,
We greet You with the washing of hands,
We greet You with our dawn fire.
Shekinah of the morning star, Shekinah of the dew,
We welcome You as the running deer,
Our feet swift in dancing.
We welcome You as the golden eagle,
Our hands spread in prayer.
We welcome You as the shimmering stream,
Our spirit flowing to the sea of Your delight.
We bless the day with our rising smoke.
Let our prayers ascend to the skies.
Let our prayers touch the earth.
Shalom Achoti, shalom Sister,
All life sings Your song."

A Meditation on the Feminine Nature of Shekinah

LYNN GOTTLIEB

Shekinah is She Who Dwells Within,
The force that binds and patterns creation.
She is Birdwoman, Dragonlady, Queen of the Heavens,
Opener of the Way.
She is Mother of the Spiritworld, Morning and Evening Star,
Dawn and Dusk.
She is Mistress of the Seas, Tree of Life,
Silvery Moon, Fiery Sun.
All these are Her names.
Shekinah is Changing Woman, Nature herself,
Her own Law and Mystery.
She is cosmos, dark hole, fiery moment of beginning.
She is dust cloud, nebulae, the swirl of galaxies.
She is gravity, magnetic field,
the paradox of waves and particles.
Shekinah is unseen dark, invisible web,
Creatrix of complex systems,
expanding, contracting, spiraling, meandering,
The beginning of Wisdom.
Shekinah is Grandmother, Grandfather, Unborn Child.
Shekinah is life loving itself into being.
Shekinah is the eros of life, limitless desire,
Cosmic orgasm, wave upon wave of arousal,
hungry and tireless, explosive and seductive,
the kiss of life and death, never dying.
Shekinah is home and hearth, root and rug,
the altar on which we light our candles.
We live here, in Her body.

She feeds multitudes from Her flesh,
Water, sap, blood, milk, fluids of life, elixir of the wounded.
Shekinah is the catalyst of our passion,
Our inner Spiritfire, our knowledge of self-worth,
Our call to authenticity.
She warms our hearts, ignites our vision.
She is the great turning round,
breathing and pulsating, pushing life toward illumination.
Womb and Grave, End and Beginning.
All these are her names.

Poem for the Shechina

CASSIA BERMAN

Holy Shechina,
    are You that gentle female Voice
    I've loved since I heard You
    speak from within me
    after waiting so long
    to hear the Voice of God I thought would be
        booming and male
    the Voice that frightened Samuel when he was a child
        in the Temple,
    whom I thought, when I was a child, would frighten me,
    the Voice of Awe of the Prophets and Mt. Sinai?
    When I first heard You,
    I knew I'd come home
    and that home was within.
Are you the Heart of the Mother,
    loving, weeping,
    nurturing, impassive,
    forgiving
    through a history soaked in the blood of Your children?
    When I asked You about that
        You told me all children die
        and are born and die and are born and die
        and are born once more—
        that's how it is on this Earth
        and You've watched it so long.
Holy Shechina,
    they say You were exiled from the world
    when God created it,
    creating separation from formless Light

but that You return once a week for 24 hours
bringing Peace and Harmony—
the Bride of our hearts
    that long to love and be loved
    why do You only come on Shabbos?
the Bride of our souls
    who are so confused in a world that turns Glory
    to death and deceit.
Holy Shechina,
    why do You only come on Shabbos?
    Are You the *Shalom* our prayers extol?
    Are You the secret of wholeness
    hidden in this long sad story we've had to live through?
Holy Shechina,
    is the reason we've had to live through it
    simply that we forgot to call You Mother,
    forgot that God in His Genderlessness
    is female too,
    and in His Omnipotence
    would treat His Bride,
        the Source of Life
    with more respect than men do—
    forgot that if we had the strength
    to welcome You every instant
        and I'm not sure we do
    You'd stay?
Holy Shechina,
    legend has it
    that if everyone on Earth on one day
    celebrated Shabbos
    Messiah would come—
    such Peace would come to every heart
    that the world as we know it
    would be undone.

Shechina,
>is the real purpose for which God created us
>to celebrate Shabbos every moment—
>to receive You,
>>our Mother,
>>our Bride,
>>the very beauty of our Selves
>>without fear, without shame,
>>without hiding,
>in every part of our being,
>always,
>forever?
>If we let You into our lives
>and honored Life without hatred
>and Love without our own ideas about it
>would You stay?

EVE 🖊

Eve Falling

JANE MCVEIGH

I love the Fall, I love the endless tumbling
of leaves over my head,
leaves of amber and grief,
leaves promising everything, even the end.
I love the way Icarus floats to the ground
splayed out like a rubber hero,
I love what he sees
the red tile roofs, the gardens,
the open mouths of the woman,
all of it rushing at him.
I love what my eyes see as I fall
into love,
the same rush, the same play
of color and wet light.

I love the Fall of man,
the way it begins with a woman's mouth.
I love my own mouth beginning to say
the truth and then the silence, the aftershock,
I love the fall of presidents and kings,
the mad fall from power into a woman's arms.

I love the way stars arc into darkness,
I love how you can't catch it,
the moment when the fall ends,
and a dream begins,
how some falling is bottomless,
I love Eve's tumbling into a world of shadows,

the shadows of leaves
as they hover and deepen and drop,
a hallelujah of color covering the ground.
I love the melting of wings,
the juice sliding down Eve's chin,
how it lands on her breast,
how she sees her breast and names it,

so that what has been body
is suddenly parts exposed,
I love how her hand falls
between her legs, how little
she hides before he enters her,
how she suddenly knows
he too has found a separate name.

She feels the quick bite of regret
but it is too late.
The snake has thickened within her brain,
wrapped itself so carefully it seems
a strand of her own thought.

I love the Fall, the way we are eased
out of Paradise gradually.
The way we begin floating
and give in so slowly to the earth.
I love the way it ends, and keeps ending.

Loba as Eve

DIANE DI PRIMA

> I am Thou & Thou art I
> and where Thou art I am
> and in all things am I dispersed
>
> and from wherever Thou willst
> Thou gatherest Me
>
> but in gathering Me
> Thou gatherest Thyself
> —GOSPEL OF EVE

i am thou & thou art i

where tossing in grey sheets you weep
I am
where pouring like mist you
                    scatter among the stars
I shine
where in black oceans of sea & sky
            you die
            you die
I chant
a voice like angels from the heart
of virgin gold,
            plaint of the unicorn caught
in the boundless circle

                    where you confront
broken glass, lost trees & men
                              tossed up
on my beaches, hear me pray:
                              your words
slip off my tongue, I am pearl
of yr final tears, none other
than yr flesh, though it go soft

I am worm
              in the tight bud, burst
of starcloud that covers your dream & morning
I am sacred mare grazing
              in meadow of yr spirit & you run
in my wind. Hear the chimes
that break from my eyes like infants
struggling eternally against
                    these swaddling clothes

and where thou art, I am

astride the wind. or held
by two hoodlums under a starting truck.
crocheting in the attic.
striding forever out of the heart of quartz
immense, unhesitant, monotonous
as galaxies; or rain; or
lost cities of the dinosaurs now sunk
in the unopening rock.

who keeps the bats from flying in your window?
who rolls the words you drop back into seed?
                        who picks
sorrows like lice from your heart & cracks them
                              between her teeth?
who else blows down your chimney with the moon
scattering ashes from your dismal hearth to show
the sleeping Bird in the coals, or is it
garnet you lost?

                      What laughter spins you
around in the windy street?

& in all things I am dispersed

gold fleece on the hunted deer.
the Name of everything.
sweet poison eternally churned
from the milky ocean.
futurity's mirror.   ivory gate
of death.
the fruit I hold out spins
the dharma wheel.
I weep
I weep
dry water I am, cold fire, "our"
Materia, mother & matrix
                    eternally in labor.
The crescent I stand on rocks
like a shaky boat, it is
the winking eye of God.

& from wherever thou willst thou gatherest me

steel, from the belly of Aries.
Or that cold fire which plays
above the sea.
White sow munching acorns in graveyards where roots
of oaks wrap powdery bones of the devas.
There, suckle at my tits. Crucify
me like a beetle on yr desk. Nod out
amidst the rustling play of lizards, recognize
epics the lichen whisper, read twigs
& leaves as they fall.

Nurture my life with quartz & alabaster
& drink my blood from a vein in my lower leg.
I neigh, I nuzzle you, I explode
          your certain myth.
I crawl slimy from a cave beneath yr heart
I hiss, I spit oracles at yr front door
in a language you have forgotten. I unroll
the scroll of yr despair, I bind yr children with it.

It is for this you love me.
It is for this
you seek me everywhere.

Because I gave you apples out of season
Because I gnaw on the boundaries of the light

but in gathering me thou gatherest thyself

daystar that hovers
over the heavy waters of that Sea
bright stone that fell
out of the fiery eye of the pyramid

it grows
out of the snake as out of the crescent:
apple you eternally devour
forever in your hand. I lock
the elements around you where you walk:

> earth from my terror
> water from my grief
> air my eternal flight
> & fire / my lust

I am child who sings
uninjured in the furnace of your flesh.

Blue earth am I & never on this earth
have I been naked
Blue light am I that runs
like marrow in the thin line of yr breath

I congeal
waterlilies on the murky pond
I hurl
the shafts of dawn like agony
                          down the night

A Prayer to Eve

KATHLEEN NORRIS

Mother of fictions
and of irony,
help us to laugh.

Mother of science
and the critical method,
keep us humble.

Muse of listeners,
hope of interpreters,
inspire us to act.

Bless our metaphors,
that we might eat them.

Help us to know, Eve,
the one thing we must do.

Come with us, muse of exile,
mother of the road.

SOPHIA 🖋

Wisdom Is

MAKEDA, QUEEN OF SHEBA
CA. 1000 BCE

Wisdom is
sweeter than honey,
brings more joy
than wine,
illumines
more than the sun,
is more precious
than jewels.
She causes
the ears to hear
and the heart to comprehend.

I love her
like a mother,
and she embraces me
as her own child.
I will follow
her footprints
and she will not cast me away.

Sophia

JOYCE RUPP

Sophia,
to you I come:
you are the Wisdom of God
you are the Whirl of the Spirit
you are the Intimate Connection
you are the Star in my Heart

Sophia,
open my being to the radiance of your presence
to the guidance of your companionship
to the compassion of your indwelling
to the lighting of your blessed vision

Sophia, trusted friend, beloved companion,
Sophia,
mercy-maker, truth-bearer, love-dweller,
Sophia,
all goodness resides within you

Sophia,
take me by the hand
bless the frailty of my weak places
strengthen my ability to dwell in darkness
for it is there that your deepest secrets are revealed

Sophia,
we walk together!

Wisdom shines bright

WISDOM OF SOLOMON 6:12–16
Today's English Version

Wisdom shines bright and never grows dim; those who love her and look for her can easily find her. She is quick to make herself known to anyone who desires her. Get up early in the morning to find her and you will have no problem; you will find her sitting at your door. To fasten your attention on Wisdom is to gain perfect understanding. If you look for her, you will soon find peace of mind, because she will be looking for those who are worthy of her, and she will find you wherever you are. She is kind and will be with you in your every thought.

Happy he who has found wisdom

PROVERBS 2:13–18
New English Bible

Happy he who has found wisdom,
and the man who has acquired understanding;
for wisdom is more profitable than silver,
and the gain she brings is better than gold.
She is more precious than red coral,
and all your jewels are no match for her.
Long life is in her right hand,
in her left hand are riches and honour.
Her ways are pleasant ways
and all her paths lead to prosperity.
She is a staff of life to all who grasp her,
and those who hold her fast are safe.

Let Wisdom Wear the Crown: Hymn for Gaia

ELSA GIDLOW

When the Wise Woman wears the crown
Marvels innumerable come to pass:
The sun rises in the East;
Seeds, well sown, swell,
Bring forth grass,
Oaks, lilies.
                Earth's children moan
In grief; laugh when they are glad.
Wonders and marvels come to pass
When the Wise Woman wears the crown.

Water flows down hill,
Finds its level on the plain
When the Wise Woman is queen.
Tigers and wolves kill
And none is moved to complain
If mild nourish fierce.

                As frost is chill
And fire burns, babes grow into women,
Sage and Child laugh, fear no bane
And find no thing to be ill.

The heart, untaught, moves the blood;
Sap of love quickens male flower
To seek female rose, rose to receive.
Unguided, the new-born knows its food.

The eye sees. Brain feels its particular power
As bare stalk knows when to bud
And death to come in its time.
Marvels, marvels, miraculous dower
And plenitude of incalculable good—

We know these to be ours,
We sing, dance on the green,
When Wisdom wears the crown,
When the Wise Woman is queen.

In the beginning

Miriam Therese Winter

In the beginning,
Wisdom:
with God,
within God
eternally.
From the beginning,
Wisdom is
God.

Through Her
all life
came to be,
born of Her light
and Her darkness
and Her rich diversity.

Into the midst of Her world,
She came,
mingled among Her own.
She came,
calling us by name.
She came
to those who would receive her.

Wisdom
made flesh
Her dwelling place,
gives
from Her fullness
grace

upon grace,
intuitively
lives
in the hollow space
within
as in
the beginning.

NUT 🖋

Hymn to Nut

ANONYMOUS

O my mother Nut,
Stretch your wings over me,
Let me become like the imperishable stars,
May Nut extend her arms over me
And her name
She Who Extends Her Arms,
Chases Away the Shadows,
And Makes the Light Shine
Everywhere.

The Loba Addresses the Goddess / or The Poet as Priestess Addresses the Loba-Goddess

DIANE DI PRIMA

Is it not in yr service that I wear myself out
running ragged among these hills, driving children
to forgotten movies?   In yr service
broom & pen. The monstrous feasts
we serve the others on the outer porch
(within the house there is only rice & salt)
And we wear exhaustion like a painted robe
I & my sisters
     wresting the goods from the niggardly
      dying fathers
healing each other w/ water & bitter herbs

that when we stand naked in the circle of lamps
(beside the small water, in the inner grove)
we show
no blemish, but also no superfluous beauty.
It has burned off in watches of the night.
O Nut, O mantle of stars, we catch at you
  lean   mournful
   ragged   triumphant
    shaggy as grass
our skins ache of emergence / dark o' the moon

PALEOLITHIC GODDESSES ❧

Mother Dawning
JANINE CANAN

In the room the women come and go
talking not of Michelangelo.
In the room the women come and go
talking of Our Lady of Brassempouy
(Hers the first face lifted from mud);
Our Lady of Grimaldi, Dordogne,
Laussel with crescent and belly;
Our Lady of Willendorf, Dolni Vestonice,
Los Angeles and Malta;
Our Lady of Africa, Asia, America, Europe,
beyond the world and worlds.

In the room where fluorescent light bulbs squeal,
the women come and go talking ecstatically
of Her of amber, bone and ivory,
Her to whom Enheduanna sang
five thousand years ago—
She who perched upon the caves
hundreds of thousands of years,
whose body is Earth and Sky,
creation's ever-changing dream.
Oh, Mother Dawning, the women cry,
Welcome, long-awaited Belonging!

Lady of Pazardzik

STARR GOODE

It was nearly seven thousand years ago
in Central Bulgaria
that an artist
took the earthy clay into her hands
and sculpted a pregnant goddess,
then placed her in the temple oven,
perhaps with a prayer
for the fields,
fertile and moist.

Now you are enthroned on my desk,
face tilted up,
hands resting on the divine belly.
As I sit before you, I am nauseated,
a waste dump site like so much of the Earth now.
I do not trust anything.
Still, the moon began again last night.
If I pulled down the copper blinds and rested in the dark,
if I placed you upon my patch of dark hair,
would you love me always as only a spirit could do?
Would I feel a pulse rise from a coiled damp place?
Lady of Pazardzik,
what is behind those thumbprint eyes?
I touch you as if I were blind.
My late start makes the day fall down all around me.
Will you carry me over the sacred sown fields,
wet fields of imagination?
Sprout me, grow me, let me ripen,
but most of all, use me for something!
        Use me

Power of the Soul

SHEILAH GLOVER

I am the snake-woman kneeling at Knossos
Riding the bull with her horns to the sky
I am the Sybil who babbles your destiny
Over the vapors at Delphi
I am Aditi, the Goddess of Nothingness
Empty and full with each phase of the moon
I am the crone who talks to the flowers
And heals your wounds

When did you come to fear and despise me
Sharpen your daggers to seize control
Five thousand years as king of the mountain
You wonder how you lost your soul

Now I'm the woman who's raped and discarded
Baby girl left on the mountain to die
Because I bleed and live close to the Earth
As I create life

When will we learn to see life together
Weaving the fragments into a whole
Moving beyond the world of power
To the power of the soul

I am the whisper that calls you in silence
I am the tear that rolls down your cheek
I am the path to the passionate river of life you seek

I pray that we learn to see life together
Weaving the fragments into a whole
Moving beyond the world of power
To the power of the soul

Venus of Laussel

PATRICIA MONAGHAN

You rise in my dreams
like the power of stone,
breaking the glass door
between wind and the body.
You are the measurer:
blood of my moons,
lines of my years.
A thread of breath
connects me to time,
wind in my blood,
a thread to your womb,
Thirteen short lines—

You rise, then are gone.

Madonna of the Peaches

JOAN SLESINGER LOGGHE

I said,
take my belly
in the peaches.

We stood amid bees
before the blossoms blew
turned brown, then into fruit.

And I was all belly
turned this way
and that in the leaves.

Photos so young and taut
smooth surface like a globe
like a pink balloon before the party.

Like Venus of Laussel
on Kodak paper. My moment
amid the spring buzzing.

I said, leave out my face
with its traces of worry
and gray hair.

But my hand on my belly,
my left hand older than peach trees,
my workaday hand.

Those veins give shadow
to a presence, ancient
closer to the Goddess.

THE GREEKS

Demeter

GENEVIEVE TAGGARD

In your dream you met Demeter
Splendid and severe, who said: Endure.
Study the art of seeds,
The nativity of caves.
Dance your gay body to the poise of waves;
Die out of the world to bring forth the obscure
Into blisses, into needs.
In all resources
Belong to love. Bless,
Join, fashion the deep forces,
Asserting your nature, priceless and feminine.
Peace, daughter. Find your true kin.
                    —then you felt her kiss.

Demeter's Blessing

Burleigh Mutén

Here is the lantern and the key.
Walk straight through the forest
to the granite cliff. Behind two
grandmother firs, you will find
the entrance to the cave, and
when you can no longer see,
follow the wall
with your hand.
Save your light for utter darkness.
And be sure to leave a flame in
the jar when you light the lamp.

Keep a reserve, daughter.
Always keep a reserve.

Here is the offering you will give
to the Father of Death who dwells
deep within our Mother. As soon
as he smiles, open your palms,
bow more slowly than ever before
and remember

he is at home in the dark
where you will be only a voice
for a time. Soon enough
you will hear the stirring within
that will grow into the prince
who will crown you as Mother,
my sister. Rejoice!

Then, only then
as the Queen of the Shades
who brought life to the land of the Dead
will you hear the key singing
in the gate where I wait.

I will open every leaf on each tree
and all flowers, seeds, and fruit will swell
as you show me the dance you have learned.

Persephone's Journey

PATRICIA MONAGHAN

I lay at rest in the violet-fragrant
meadow, that other world of
honey sun and maiden beauty,
nothing moving, nothing moving
except the bees penetrating
the narcissus near my hand,
except the catkins swaying
in the wind-touched willow,
except the sparrows, the sparrows
with their bright dancing song.

That was my world then:
peace, I thought, perfection,
yes, perfection, the sun warm
against my skin and the breezes
in my hair and the sap rising
in the red-gold dogwood, in
the green alder, in the willow thicket.

The sap was rising in me
too. I did not know it, I did not
know that I was waiting, waiting,
coiled like a snake or a fern's frond,
curled tight against myself, ready to
shed myself, ready to unfurl,
ready—

He arrived like an earthquake.
He arrived like a storm on
spring leaves. He arrived like

a great hawk from a vacant sky.
He arrived like an antlered
deer by a waterfall. He arrived
like a wolf from the hills.

I felt myself break apart.
I felt like a continent set loose
to drift upon the ocean. I felt
like a comet in cold space.
I felt like the first horse,
the first horsewoman.
I felt like new fire.

My soul flew out through my eyes
like a tiny bird, my soul flew out
through my eyes like a butterfly.

The world disappeared.
Yes, the world disappeared.
And I did not care.
He led me to a place
I had seen in dreams,
a place where blue
winds ripped across
a cold mountain pass
and tiny asters
starred from gray rock
and the universe flowed
and flowered and flamed.

He took me to places silent
and precise, pastures where
grass rippled like muscle,
where bees alit on flowers
still as carvings, where
impermanence was graven
into time and flesh became

stone, became crystal, became
star's metal, became obsidian.

I became transformed.
My hands became eyes.
My eyes became hands.
My breasts became mouths.
My mouth became a beast,
a ravening beast, a famished
and ravishing beast.

He was an eagle above me,
a whale beneath me, he was
a distant asteroid, he was
alien and beautiful.
I breathed in his difference
like violet flowers.
I bathed in his difference
as in the oil of almonds.

And so I took his seed.
I took it inside me.
And not just once.

He was a pomegranate,
all leathery ripe flesh,
and I took every seed,
every red kernel,
every fragment of him.
I could not stop.
I would not stop.
I did not stop.
And then I left him.

I left him because I remembered
meadows where eyes did not peer
from every leaf. I remembered hills

where the hands of trees did not
stroke me as I passed. I remembered
solitude. I remembered myself.

I remembered a wild northern
lake in spring. I remembered it
in my blood, in my mouth.

It had been easy to go with him.
It was not easy to leave. The world
seemed dry and cold. The world

seemed empty. But I walked
away from his fire and
his knowledge, into my own.

I walked until I saw sharp peaks
and sheep climbing on sharp
hooves into slanting sunlight.

I walked until I saw an eagle rise
from a dead tree beside a river
that braided itself into a lake.

Persephone, to Demeter

MARILYN KRYSL

Mother, I'll
tell you. Let me tell you it's
easy, going down in the
dark. I take all the right drugs,
not too much, not too little, I'm

    careful. I count the stone
        steps: one at a
            time. Each step taking me

deeper, my feet
    repeating, and I listen
        to my breathing, the piston
            thrust, back and forth,

of my breath. My fingertips
    pull along the stone
        wall. It's something to
        feel. Then I see the first star

for the last time. I look down
for good. The seconds iron links
I am forging, making a vast mail,
a chain, and there isn't any
pain: Mother, it feels like

nothing at all. I proceed at a steady
crawl, each step a dull
thud. I have your iron
in my blood. And soon enough

I arrive. He asks after
your health, takes my hand like a father, a distant

brother. Mother, there's not much
to eat, but down here I don't
care. No fruit, a thin, red
wine. A white
bed. I

sleep. The rest
is easy. You know the rest. I'm
not allowed out, I may not
seem busy. No knitting, no purling,
no throwing myself into the
piano, there

isn't one. I pass time in the same
room with him, stare at the wall,
let him think I'm thinking of
him. A tight schedule of silence,
punctual meals. Waiting it out,

biting my nails, Mother,
listen: it's coming back that isn't
easy. There's nothing worse than having to
retrace memory. Erase
iron. I have to

erase iron: think of it, Mother,
trying to pry loose all the little
links in the blood, one at a time, and climb

uphill, carrying my own image,
his gift to you and yours
to him:
        a daughter, the reminder
that this is hell
the two of you made
together. I am
the struck bargain, the go
between. I go

between the narrow walls, up the damp
stairs, not a spiral but straight up,
and I sweat, approaching your heat,
I hear water, laughter, the piano
and you. Mother, it

hurts. It hurts to be your
daughter, I didn't know if I could
do it, I thought I might
die, aching toward
your voice, calling *summer, come here*
    summer,
        my foot on the next to the last
           tread—and then you said

daughter.
       Daughter, you say,
standing in the lighted
doorway, letting the scissors
fall from your hand. Mother, it

hurts,
pulled up into
scalding light, it hurts to look
in your eyes again, to get
well again, to keep
climbing up out of hell again

and again. Mother, it hurts
the way the foot, unbound, rips apart
as the blood, streaming back,
screams down its track. Mother,
I tell you, it hurts. But Mother,

I'm back.

Persephone

KATHLEEN NORRIS

I was not a good daughter;
I coveted the cool of dark
after sun-brilliant days,
and dreamed of spiraling to the stars.

He saw me and desired me
and took me to unimagined night.
I was afraid at first
and mourned my sweet flowers.
But I learned to eat
what was put before me,
and became a wife.

My mother raged, my husband
capitulated. When the deal was struck
no one thought I'd be torn in two.

Now I have my pied-à-terre
and the inner darkness.
Sometimes I think it comes to nothing.

Now spring is a blind green wall.

Persephone

ZIPORAH HILDEBRANDT

The taste of pomegranate
betrays me; my stained teeth,
fingers, lips. Do you see
the dust of day's eyes
in my hair? I picked them
dew-laden, gold and white.
Brown hills, brown grass.
Show me your asphodels.
I can weep no longer
for my daisies.

Demeter's Song

STARHAWK

I am the wealthy one,
I am the wealthy one,
All that I have I give to you
Blossom and bud
The leaf and the promise of fruit to come
The corn and the wheat
The grass and the earth beneath your feet.

I am the wealthy one,
I am the wealthy one,
All that you have I give to you
Rhythm and form,
The lover's smile and the worker's arm,
Your blood and your breath
Pleasure and sorrow, birth and death.

I am the wealthy one,
I am the wealthy one,
All that I am I am in you
The change that frees
The heart that cries and the hand that heals
The eye that sees true
Power to destroy and to renew.

I am the wealthy one,
I am the wealthy one,
All that I am I am in you.

Queen Medusa
BURLEIGH MUTÉN

Here I sing of the Muses
    who gift the Earth
    with vision and voice
    and of their cousin,
        Fair Medusa
of the shining gold wings.

Hallowed healer whose
wisdom has been hidden
lo! these eons, turn now,
show the crown of
deathchange and rebirth
that sits upon your serpent hair.
    Show the strong beauty
    that has always been yours,
    Queen of the Deep Sea,
    Queen of the deep, red blood.

The dark moon widens
    to a crescent smile
    low on the horizon
        Mother of Pegasus,
        I welcome you.

Apotheosis of Medusa

PAT PARNELL

Flaming with anger and despair, Perseus is hunting Medusa. His
newly sharpened sword gleaming, he runs shouting through
the city streets. "Where are you, you snake charmer! I will
destroy you as you have destroyed me!" He has been
drinking.

In the park in front of the cathedral, Medusa, young and beautiful
again, sits cross-legged on a great rock playing her flute, her
golden robe wrapped round her. Three of her snakes have
braided themselves into a crown for her wine-dark hair. Two,
with green and purple scales shining, interlock in a caduceus
on an oak sapling before her, their coupling timed to the
rhythm of her music. Her other snakes circle around them,
swaying half-erect to her song.

Suddenly Perseus is there, enraged. "You have ruined my life, you
and your youth and beauty." The circus has dismissed him,
telling him he is too old for Medusa. Him, the greatest sword
swallower of all time—replaced with a handsome young fire-
eater! "What can I do? Where can I go?" He is sobbing with
fear and hatred. Eternity confronts him, empty, aimless. "You
tricked me. But I'll get even. You and your slimy snakes."
He has always hated them. "Now I'll finish what I started so
long ago."

Medusa rises, her serpent crown uncoiling. Protecting her, her
snakes are a hissing army, heads back, fangs bared. Perseus
attacks in frenzy. Blinded by bloodlust he does not see Medusa
disappear against the shrubbery.

With the serpents shredded at his feet, Perseus turns his bloody
sword toward Medusa. Where is she? "Snake Woman!" With

a great cry, Perseus rushes in search of her, hacking the underbrush.

Quickly Medusa gathers her bloodied companions into her robe. Where to hide? The open doors of the cathedral beckon like the entrance to her cave.

Inside, she hears a soft call, "Come to me, Snake Woman." Halfway down one side of the vast darkness, a soft light gleams, the sanctuary of Mary, Queen of Heaven. Her great statue wears a blue robe and a crown of stars. Her serpent is beneath her heel. Candles flicker in the darkness around her, and the statue glows softly from within. "Cast your friends before me," Mary says. "I will heal them." Rejoined, the snakes curl at the statue's feet, and Medusa's robe gleams golden, cleansed.

"Snake Woman, are you here?" Perseus's great cry fills the cathedral. "Come," says Mary, holding out a hand. "I am Queen of Snake Goddesses. I will hide you." She draws Medusa up into the statue as Perseus, sword ready, rushes past.

Medusa has found a home. The statue is hollow, airy, much larger on the inside than out. The smooth plaster walls work like one-way glass: all that happens in the cathedral is a panorama for Medusa. She sleeps coiled in the base of the statue. There is even room for her to play her flute. Her snakes are happy to stay curled with the painted one at Mary's feet.

Sometimes at night Mary and Medusa fly together hand in hand through the heavens, visiting Mary's realm. The sky is full of snakes. Ophiucus, the Serpent-Bearer, with his writhing Serpens, greets them; Aesclepius, who learned from serpents how to revive the dead; the fire-breathing Draco, swishing his double tail, rears to hug Medusa as they fly by, heading for Perseus's constellation in the northern sky. The Eye of the Medusa mask winks at them as they buzz around the starry hero like a pair of mosquitoes, teasing. Perseid meteors shower them with stardust as they head home.

Perseus, earthbound, lives in the homeless shelter in the cathedral basement, peeling potatoes and washing dishes for his keep. His sword chops sausages for the cabbage soup. He spends his mornings searching the park for Medusa, his afternoons in prayer before the statue of the Virgin. He does not see all the snake eyes staring at him below the blue robe. Medusa is near, somewhere, he is sure, he feels her presence, but always she eludes him. Sometimes he thinks he hears her flute, but he pushes that fantasy firmly away.

One day a cleaning woman, in great agitation, reports a miracle to the cathedral administrator. "There are extra snakes at the feet of the Blessed Virgin. Her statue glows from within. And I heard music playing." The cleric doesn't bother to check. "Too much *vino*," he decides, and transfers her to cleaning toilets. The other cleaning women keep silent. They know what they know. And when they have carefully dusted the snakes—and the starry crown—they kneel before the Queen of Heaven a few extra moments in silent prayer.

The Muse as Medusa

MAY SARTON

I saw you once, Medusa; we were alone.
I looked you straight in the cold eye, cold.
I was not punished, was not turned to stone—
How to believe the legends I am told?

I came as naked as any little fish,
Prepared to be hooked, gutted, caught;
But I saw you, Medusa, made my wish,
And when I left you I was clothed in thought . . .

Being allowed, perhaps, to swim my way
Through the great deep and on the rising tide,
Flashing wild streams, as free and rich as they,
Though you had power marshaled on your side.

The fish escaped to many a magic reef;
The fish explored many a dangerous sea—
The fish, Medusa, did not come to grief,
But swims still in a fluid mystery.

Forget the image: your silence is my ocean,
And even now it teems with life. You chose
To abdicate by total lack of motion,
But did it work, for nothing really froze?

It is all fluid still, that world of feeling
Where thoughts, those fishes, silent, feed and rove;
And, fluid, it is also full of healing,
For love is healing, even rootless love.

I turn your face around! It is my face.
That frozen rage is what I must explore—
Oh secret, self-enclosed, and ravaged place!
This is the gift I thank Medusa for.

Her Story

Leah Korican

1

Into your trunk
a curved woman's body is carved.
You are faceless,
swelling belly polished smooth
by palm and cheek.
I chew your bitter, brittle leaves,
seek and find
my sea blue mind.
At your roots I offer
clear green stones,
clay animals, roses, figs.
I offer olive oil, garlic, honey wine.
I bring bells, iridescent feathers,
and silk squares, printed with prayers.
I offer pennies, chocolate bars,
drawings on matchbook covers,
old melons, egg shells, coffee grounds,
compost.
I sit at your foot,
sing into the air.
I bring my breath, bones, and hair
to you, O Daphne,
your presence filled with fragrance.

2

A nearby island blown to bits.
Lava streamed red

hissed into steaming white foam.
Here the ground heaved and split,
the sea, a single wall of water
pounding into the cliffs.
Did the earth convulse at his approach?
Or was our calamity simply his opportunity?
Was he the fire that feeds on dry wood
or a comet with a blinding tail?
Warnings, disasters
followed by the conqueror
and his god, Apollo.

They say he tried to win my heart,
but he had already taken, with his lance,
all, but my compliance.
They say he loved me for my beauty,
wanted to tame me,
comb my unkempt hair.
He preferred
to twist my braid in his fist.
His was no arrow pierced heart.
He was the stabber,
but I am no scabbard for his fleshy sword.

I ran to the river's source
planted my feet into the mud.
I ran to the laurel tree,
reached up for her sky bound boughs.
At his touch I became wood.
He cannot penetrate
my smooth bark.
At his touch my body grew
hundreds of limbs,
mouth sealed over.
My screams the scent of bay.

He may crown victory with my leaves,
but he never entered my damp core.
He may crown poets with my stems,
I chant my songs into their dreams.
My roots are deep, and I am patient,
as wood grain,
as winter rain,
as women.

3

Hail Daphne
full of pains,
You are every woman telling this story.
Told on the phone or to a friend of a friend
in passing. Told
in black, bold headlines.
In a whisper or a moan.

You said across the table
how he hit and raped and beat you.
You held the smooth cup in your hand
the familiar gold bangles
on your bronze wrist.

I heard you on TV,
in the sweet voice of a virgin,
telling how her father's hero
held her down.

You told me
sitting in a quiet stone courtyard
how he followed your old mother home
and raped her, in her own doorway.

You mentioned your high school teacher
how he taught you girls

are only for one thing
after a field trip,
in the back seat of his car.

You told me on national TV,
under the gaze of accusing senators.
You told me in a calm voice,
in an even tone.
Your strength was palpable
as a thick trunk
which I could wrap my arms
around and smell the perfume
of your leaves.

4

A spell for the violators

May they be transformed.
May their spirits become warm milk.
May their hearts become smooth beach glass.
May their hands become two grassy hills.
May their minds become snow.
May they become small birds, stars, fir trees,
food for the hungry.
May they know power without violence.
Sex without force.
Love without malice.
The chalice in the heart.

5

A prayer for the survivors

May your scars be washed in warm milk.
May your courage be carved on monuments.
May your tears grow into redwoods.

May your rage be a fierce wind.
May your sex be the open sky.
May your heart be a whole mountain.
May your stories become the logs
that dam the flood of violence
and the silence of wood
become the voice of power.

Queen Hera
BURLEIGH MUTÉN

Long ago before the wars
Hera was our Mother,
goddess of the air married to the land.
She had no reason to be angry.
She had no rapist brother–husband
who tied women's wrists
to the branches of trees
suspending what was sacred about women
long ago before the wars.

Robed in deep maroon and crowned with
wild willow and lily of the valley,
Queen Hera held our mothers
as they opened to hold us.
All her daughters' newborn babies
were cared for by her priestess matrons
while Hera Herself carried
our mothers to the river
where she bathed them
and praised their courage
and their strength to carry on
the mystery of bearing spirits
to the Earth. And she did this
for us, remember? when
it was our turn to open.

Early in the spring
beneath the setting circle moon at dawn
we gathered, remember? in a long
silent line carrying our shields

and wearing double crescent moons
like horns on our heads,
breathing carefully
as the direction of the light
changed from west to east.
And at the first sight of the circle sun
lifting into the sky Herself
we began to move forward, one after the other
through the streets and out through the meadows
to the stadium on the mountainside
where we opened our chests fully
to sing celebration of our mother
and our own fertile mothering,
forming the first circle of women,
the women who watched the moon and sun
and could see the delicate differences
of the tiny leaves of plants and knew
which ones would nourish pregnancy and
which ones, leaves or seeds,
boiled or from the vine
could bring on bleeding rivers
to wash away the spirits that came too soon.

Remember when we counted our years
by the number of first circle festivals
we'd participated in, remembering
each year throughout the next
by who raced on foot
or drew the archer's bow
or who wove the banners
or placed the fire circle stones?
When I was just a girl tending
the youngest who could walk,
I wanted more than anything
to take a turn as harpist.

Queen Hera sat with arms outstretched
on a throne of ivory and gold
a deep red pomegranate
in the palm of one hand,
and atop her scepter in the other
perched the cuckoo,
two widespread peacocks at her side.
Remember how she found the eyes
of each of us and nodded,
tilting the benign rays of the sun
onto our faces radiant with the glimpse
of She Who Makes Glad
and She Who Makes the Seasons Turn
and All the Flowers Open?

Before our Queen,
we maidens ran with maidens
fleet and full of promise like the dark moon
turning toward a fullness of ourselves as
carriers of life, remember?

And we mothers stood together,
tall and strong, assured that
birth returns from death
like the slimming crescent moon turning
ever turning toward the wisdom of ourselves,
remember?
Placing our feet and hands precisely,
pulling our bowstrings
and our breath to tautness,
we let fly our arrows
straight to the heart
of any who would think to harm our young,
and we never missed our mark.

We crones, wizened with the turning
and returning of so many circle moons,

sat together near our Queen,
all the others crowded round to hear the stories
that we wove with our breath into the cool
night air, remember?
And how we cried and crowed
at the stories of before and what we've known
and what would come,
all stories carried on the voice
growing every season
long ago before the wars
when Hera was our mother,
goddess of the air married to the land.

Hymn to Aphrodite

HOMER
adapted by Patricia Monaghan

1

I sing of Aphrodite, the lover's goddess,
beautiful, gold-crowned, a blossom
riding the seafoam, resting on wind.
She comes ashore, and women
in gold bracelets meet her, bearing
silken garments for her lovely body,
copper rings for her shell ears,
chains of gold for her silver breasts.

They lead her from the seashore.
Do not look upon her! Your eyes
would dazzle from such beauty.
But you do not need to see her.
You already know her. It is she
who moves you in your dance.
She is the music of your life.
Do you need to ask her name?
Call her Love. Call her Joy.
Call her golden Aphrodite.

She is the moment when body
knits to body and the world flowers.
She enlivens everything: plants
in the meadow, the ocean's fish,
animals hidden in the forest,
birds tumbling on the wind.
She is our darling, who under

the wheeling stars makes all
things blossom and bear fruit.
At her approach storms clear,
dark clouds dissolve to blue,
sweet earth and all the oceans
smile, and her light dances brilliant
through the flourishing world.

2

She came to Ida, flowing Ida, Ida of the streams,
with grey wolves behind her and bright lions
and thick bears and quick hungry panthers.
They moved like dancers around her.
She moved like a woman in love.
And when they saw this, they grew
hot and full of longing—even animals grow
hot and full of longing in her presence—
and two by two they left her, following
each other into the valleys to mate,
their bodies hot and full of longing.
And so, we too. And so, we too.

3

The golden one has left us, gone to her island,
gone to her temple there, gone to her shrine
with its incensed altar. She has left us behind
and closed the door. If we could see her now
how beautiful she would be: imagine her there,
the Graces bathing her—those lovely handmaids—
and oiling her with fragrant sweetness, covering
every curve of her bountiful body with sacredness
and the green scent of olives, and dressing her

in filmy silken robes, and roping her neck
with golden chains, dropping gold from her ears,
ringing her fingers with gold. She is laughing.
How our darling loves to laugh! And now
look! she is leaving her temple again, coming
back to bring us more joyous trouble, laughing
and laughing, cutting a path right through the stars.

4

I will build you, goddess, an altar
high up on the mountain peak,
where everyone can see it, and each season
I will cover it with the richest offerings.
Think kindly of me therefore,
grant me a long and sunny life,
let me be happy among my loves,
and prosperous up to the ripe edge of age.

5

She has come back, piercing us all
with her sweetness, her power.
Birdsong swells, the antelope leaps
swift mountain streams, the west wind
wraps us in honeyed warmth.
She has returned, our golden one.
She moves laughing through our world
and we follow her. Through the forest,
through the fields, across the hills,
we follow her, all of us in love,
loving each other, in love with her.
When she returns, it is always summer.
Don't you hear the swallows and cicadas?

Don't you hear the nightingale?
Don't you hear the brooks running silver,
the rivers running darkly to the sea?
Don't you hear the whole world singing
her praises? Everything is singing, everyone
is in love, because our goddess has come home.

It's no use

Verse 12

SAPPHO

translated by Mary Barnard

It's no use

Mother dear, I
can't finish my
weaving
      You may
blame Aphrodite

soft as she is

she has almost
killed me with
love for that boy

Prayer to my lady of Paphos

Verse 38

SAPPHO
translated by Mary Barnard

Dapple-throned Aphrodite,
eternal daughter of God,
snare-knitter! Don't, I beg you,

cow my heart with grief! Come,
as once when you heard my far-
off cry and, listening, stepped

from your father's house to your
gold car, to yoke the pair whose
beautiful thick-feathered wings

oaring down mid-air from heaven
carried you to light swiftly
on dark earth; then, blissful one,

smiling your immortal smile
you asked, What ailed me now that
made me call you again? What

was it that my distracted
heart most wanted? "Whom has
Persuasion to bring round now

"to your love? Who, Sappho, is
unfair to you? For, let her
run, she will soon run after;

"if she won't accept gifts, she
will one day give them; and if
she won't love you—she soon will

"love, although unwillingly. . . ."
If ever—come now! Relieve
this intolerable pain!

What my heart most hopes will
happen, make happen; you yourself join forces on my side!

Visit to the Palace of Venus

IRENE YOUNG

With grace she granted
me entry
over the icy earth
through the door
to the warmth
of her humble palace

There as her emerald throne
shone in the moonlight
in the sunlight
and in her light
She gifted me jewelry
gave me rose colored garb
warm enough to welcome
the coldest of nights
and honored me
with seeds of her soul

In the morning
she fed me berries
as we lounged like
two queens not needing
to change a single thing
in our queendom

My body rose
only to float down
the hallway to
blue green waters

where my spirit was bathed
and I surrendered
so deep into pleasure
that I forgot
why I was ever
so afraid to visit her

She never revealed
the power she has
to open or close
the door of her
looking glass palace
where eyes are bearers
of so much essence
that tears are as ready
to be released
as a common smile
And in all her artful gesturing
she never drew lines
between yes
no
and maybe

My palace is your palace, she said
as I took the gifts she had given and
reluctantly prepared to part
with her glorious presence

I wondered if there were
secret chambers only lovers were shown
where siren songs simultaneously
weaken and strengthen
wounded hearts
and there is no resistance
to falling in love

Would she
with grace
ever reveal them to me

Then I remembered
why I was ever
so afraid to visit her

In Hecate's Garden

ZIPORAH HILDEBRANDT

The pumpkins rove the ground,
    clambering rocks, leaping shrubbery, over and beyond.
Leaves lifted high, banners in the wind,
    drinking the sun, shading the earth.
I am pushing, running, growing as fast
Flowing on juice-energy, sprouting new buds,
    Reaching new tendrils
Right up until the frosty breath of cold limitations blasts
growth finally
    To winter's quiescence.
I am not dead for I live in what I have made,
    The house of my fruits.
I am not dead for my blossoms live in memory,
    Golden exuberant stars, much visited by bees.
I cannot die for I live too fully to repent.
I cannot cease for the motion that is my being moves
    In the electrons of galaxies.
Even in the chilled, blackened skeletons of my leaves,
In the questing thread of my desiccated vine, I speak.
And I say death and life are not essential.
I say green and orange are shapes hovering in the mind.
I say the mind is a full moon pumpkin,
    Skin, rind, seeds and hollow
    As infinite as the universe.
All of me is here, now, infinite, joyous, blessed.

from *The Hymn to the Moon*

HOMER

translated by Charles Boer

Go on,
    Muses,
and sing the Moon with her big wings,

          . . . Off her immortal head
                   a brightness
               pointed from heaven,
                        encircles earth,
          and from this brightness
                   great beauty,
          and the air
               that was unlighted before
          glows
               with her golden crown,
          and her rays spring out
          when the goddess
                   Selene
          has washed her beautiful body
          in Ocean,
          and put on her clothes
                   that shine so far
          and yoked her flashing horses
               with their strong necks,
          and when she speeds these horses on
            ·   in their beautiful hair,
          at evening,
          in the middle of the month

Her great orb is full then
and her rays, as she is
                increasing,
become brightest

            And she becomes
                an assurance
                a sign
                        to men

There was once a time
when she made love
            to Zeus
                in bed
She became pregnant
and had a daughter,
            Pandia,
            who had a particular beauty
            among the immortal gods

Greetings, lady
    goddess with white arms
    divine Selene
        kind Selene
            with your beautiful hair . . .

from *The Hymn to Hestia*

HOMER
translated by Charles Boer

Hestia,
you who have received the highest honor,
to have your seat forever
in the enormous houses of all the gods
and all the men who walk on the earth,
it is a beautiful gift you have received,
it is a beautiful honor.
Without you, mankind would have no feasts,
since no one could begin the first and last drink
of honey-like wine without an offering
to Hestia.

In the young spring evening
Verses 22–25

SAPPHO
translated by Charoula

In the young spring evening
The moon is shining full
Girls form a circle
As though round an altar

And their feet perform
Rhythmical steps
Like the soft feet of Cretan girls
Must once have danced

Round and round an altar of love
Designing a circle
In the delicate flowering grass

The stars that are shining
Around the beautiful moon
Hide their own bright faces
When She, at Her fullest
Paints the earth with Her
Silvery light

Now, while we are dancing
Come! Join us!
Sweet joy, revelry,
Bright light!

Inspire us, muses
Oh, you with the beautiful hair.

The Hesperides

BURLEIGH MUTÉN

Here I sing
of the Hesperides:
    Arethusa,
    Erytheia,
    and Aegle

hesitating   as the light
begins to quiver the shadows
signaling the evening stars.

Red deepens pushing rosy orange
streaks into pink and purple indigo.
The hour opens and widens thinning
into the other place, the Other Side.

The song of Hesperides rings out over
the opal sea panning the bright white
line that rims the edge of the world, calling
with arms inviting, intoning with eyes that
have seen every sort of death, soothing and
holding those jolted from the forms we know
into the long low light of dusk.

Urania

BURLEIGH MUTÉN

Here I sing
           of Urania
swirling
like the South Wind
placing her feet precisely
she whips past the tall stones
that ring the ritual ground
lifting lighting lifting
lighting like the night birds
gathering in the silence
watching her trace the pattern
of the stars arcing overhead.
She calls the Moon
to crest this high horizon
dancing an invocation of time:
a sliver of silver slowly
    swiftly widens
      washing the place with light.

KALI, DURGA, LAKSMI 🌿

Oh Kali

JANINE CANAN

Hi Kali, come on in.
I've been waiting for You
in this loneliness
that prefers even the company of Death
to no one—
to You alone
I bow down.

🌿

Kali, only You are great enough
to take this deafening confusion
overflowing with pain
and topped with resistance—
a dish appropriate
only for You,
Glorious Devourer.

🌿

Oh Kali, vast and voluptuous
are your flames—engulfing,
devouring, triumphant!
Only You can swallow this seething,
becoming more beautiful,
graceful and tender—
Divine Daughter, All Powerful!

❧

You who bring grief,
who destroy beauty,
who abandon lovers,
who betray human hope—
stronger and more violent than Death,
You force me open, Great One.
My heart is too small—I'm shattering—

Kali

LUCILLE CLIFTON

Kali
queen of fatality, she
determines the destiny
of things. nemesis.
the permanent guest
within ourselves.
woman of warfare,
of the chase, bitch
of blood sacrifice and death.
dread mother. the mystery
ever present in us and
outside us. the
terrible hindu woman God
Kali.
who is black.

calming Kali

LUCILLE CLIFTON

be quiet awful woman,
lonely as hell,
and i will comfort you
when i can
and give you my bones
and my blood to feed on.
gently gently now
awful woman,
i know i am your sister.

Kali

Leslie Simon

I think my friend's mother
had the right idea
when he came home at sixteen
begging for a big boy's bike—
the motorcycle mantra,
she said:
"Why don't we just save
a lot of time and money,
and I'll *kill* you right now?"

My son is almost sixteen;
he dons a helmet and rides
in and out of tight places
on city streets,
claiming his new scooter's
lack of power protects him;
tempering that young man drive,
it doesn't tempt with high speeds.

And I remember my pregnancy dreams:
with daughter, I saw multi-colored flowers
and shells, a gold vest floating;
with son, I mounted motorcycles
in dream after dream,
black and white movies;
racing, I always won.

And now this message from mother to son:
"Okay, I promise I won't kill you,
but I *will* you another kind of power,
from my dreams."

from *The Invocation to Kali*

MAY SARTON

It is time for the invocation:

Kali, be with us.
Violence, destruction, receive our homage.
Help us to bring darkness into the light,
To lift out the pain, the anger,
Where it can be seen for what it is—
The balance-wheel for our vulnerable, aching love.
Put the wild hunger where it belongs,
Within the act of creation,
Crude power that forges a balance
Between hate and love.

Help us to be the always hopeful
Gardeners of the spirit
Who know that without darkness
Nothing comes to birth
As without light
Nothing flowers.

Bear the roots in mind,
You the dark one, Kali,
Awesome power.

Kali

ZIPORAH HILDEBRANDT

Kali
my toes strike lightning
my feet thunder

Kali
my legs run with every womb-bearing creature
my belly always empty always full

Kali
my breasts every river
my arms ten thousand

Kali
my mouth devours duality, desire, despair, ignorance, suffering
my tongue slathers each cell with juicy tantric compassion

Kali
my brow bright moon wisdom shining
my crown illuminates infinite timespace

Kali
my ears hum om ma om ma om ma hum
I am all nothing nothing all

My blissful Mother exists fully through every creature!

LEX HIXON

Meditate, O mind, on the mystery of Kali.
Use any method of worship you please,
or be free from methods,
breathing day and night her living name
    as the seed of power
planted by the teacher in your heart.

Consider the simple act of lying down to sleep
    as devoted offering of body and mind to her.
Allow your dreams to become
    radiant meditations on the Cosmic Mother.
As you wander through countryside or city,
feel that you are moving through *Kali, Kali, Kali.*
All sounds you hear are her natural mantras
    arising spontaneously
as the whole universe worships her,
prostrates to her, awakens into her.

The Goddess, who is unitive wisdom,
constitutes the letters of every alphabet.
Every word secretly bears the power of her name.

The singer of this mystic hymn is overwhelmed:
"Wonderful! Wonderful! My blissful Mother
    exists fully through every creature!
O wandering poet,
whatever food or drink you receive,
offer as oblation in the sacrificial fire of your body
    and dissolve your mind
into her all-encompassing reality."

Who can keep a blazing fire tied in a cotton cloth?

Lex Hixon

My intimate companion,
why not plunge into union
    with Great Goddess Kali?
Discover your spiritual anxiety
    to be without the slightest ground.

The obscure night of your religious quest is over
    and the day of truth is dawning.
The sunlight of Mother Wisdom instantly pervades
    the landscape of awareness,
for darkness is not a substance that offers resistance.
Precious Kali, you have risen as the morning sun,
opening the lotus centers of my subtle perception
    to your naked, timeless radiance.

Proliferating systems of ritual and philosophy
    attempt to throw dust into the eyes
of the eternal wisdom that abides in every soul.
How can any system transcend the play of relativity?
But when relative existence is revealed
    as the country fair of Mother's sheer delight,
there are no teachers and nothing to teach,
no students and nothing to learn.
The actors and their lines are simply expressions
    of the Wisdom Goddess
who directs this entire drama.
Be confident that you will soon awaken fully
    as the essence of her reality!

The courageous lover tastes the bliss of the Beloved
    and enters the secret city of the Goddess,
passing beyond the threshold of ecstasy
    into the open expanse of enlightenment.

Astonished by this sudden journey,
Mother's poet now sings madly:
"My delusion is gone, gone, utterly gone!
Who can obscure truth?
Who can keep a blazing fire tied in a cotton cloth?"

Song to the Mother of the World

SUZANNE IRONBITER

Now the stars flush with joy
from their toes to their cheeks
throughout deep space.
In their choral rows,
they mirror the earth's people. All sing my praises:

"Goddess, Matarjagat,
Mother of People, Mother of the World,
Mother of dead ones and live ones,
having won out in three great wars in the hearts of men
between demons and stars,
you are Goddess of All.

"Mother of Earth,
support us,
make the world of living creatures one.

"Sea Mother,
be around us,
move us, rest us.

"Mother of Life,
breathe in us,
beat in us.
Draw forth our powers to touch and smell and taste,
to see and hear you.
Show us the ways to know you.
Let us touch your heart.

"Mother of Knowledge,
you make our life a crystal form
displaying your aspects.
It is dark by day and clear in dreamlight.

"Mother of Visions,
in your three-stranded braid, in your three eyes,
in your mighty trident prongs
you create, sustain, destroy us,
you destroy, sustain, create us.

"We cling to you, giver of refuge, constant shelter,
only companion in our sufferings,
the only one who goes with us to death.

"Your forms are endless—
Brahmani, Maheshvari, Kaumari,
Vaishnavi, Aindri,
Chamunda, Durga, Chandika, Ambika—
endless your names, your weapons, mounts, and jewels,
yet each one moves in us
and gives us power.

"May your sword,
smeared with the blood and fat of the fallen demons,
your great light gleaming in its magic steel,
be sharp for us.

"Age after age, the evils in us rise against us,
and we who were healthy grow sick and feeble.
We fear the wars to come.
We call on you, Goddess.
Save us from the powers that destroy us."

The goddess Laksmi

ANONYMOUS
translated by W. S. Merwin and J. Moussaieff Masson
ELEVENTH CENTURY CE

The goddess Laksmi
loves to make love to Vishnu
from on top
looking down she sees in his navel
a lotus
and on it Brahma the god
but she can't bear to stop
so she puts her hand
over Vishnu's right eye
which is the sun
and night comes on
and the lotus closes
with Brahma inside

Mother Lakshmi's Poem

CASSIA BERMAN

If you would give as I do,
give from the place where nothing can be taken away from you—
give from the place of the spirit.
See everything as formed from that inexhaustible spirit
for the moment that it's given, lasting as long as its purpose is.
Have faith that nothing is taken away from you
that has not outlived its purpose.
Relinquish the idea that you have anything to do with it
and in that way your clinging and self-doubt will fall away.

A Prayer to the Divine Mother

ANDREW HARVEY

for Rose Solari

O Divine Mother,
In this extreme danger,
when we and all sentient beings
and nature,
    herself,
    Your glorious body,
face unprecedented misery and destruction,
inaugurate in fierceness and tenderness
the splendor of
    Your Age of Passionate Enlightenment.
Bring us into the fire of Your sacred passion for reality,
rejoin the severed mandala of our being,
infuse our bodies, our hearts, our souls, our minds,
with the calm and focused truth of Your highest illumination
that brings each of those things into mutual harmony.
Engender in the ground of all of our beings
the sacred marriage,
that union between masculine and feminine
from which in each of us the Divine Child is born,
    that Child that is flesh of Your flesh,
        heart of Your heart,
        light of Your light,
    That Child that is free from all dogma,
        free from all shame,
        free from all false divisions
            between holy and unholy
            sacred and profane,

        free to burn out in love,
        free to play in love,
        free to serve in love,
            as love
            for love
in the heart of Your burning ground of life.
Teach us, O Divine Mother, directly
at every moment in this hour of apocalypse
the appropriate action that heals
        and preserves
        and redeems
        and transforms.

SHEILA NA GIG 🖎

Sheila the Hat
PAT PARNELL

for the Rahara Sheila, County Roscommon

Sheila-na-gig, I will make myself a hat
in your image. The fabric is grey and rough,
like the keystone in which you were carved
on the old church wall.
Your hands hold open your lips
so they fit snugly over my ears.
My head is a giant egg you are laying
or the last bit of a breech birth
that you are pushing out of yourself.

I will wear you skiing
when the bright winter sun shines blinding
off the snow.
Your lips clutch tight,
warming me with your body heat.
You crouch above my forehead, facing
into the wind, shading my eyes.
Your hands clasp under my chin,
your legs cross over my chest,
hugging close.
Your thick braids
swing across my shoulders,
thumping,
as we tuck, twist, and turn, speeding
down the slope.

The wind of our race
flattens your breasts against your rib cage.
Your Gaelic battle cry cheers me on.
Everyone who sees you will say,
"What a great hat!"

Sile Na gCioch

Pat Parnell

Let's build a ferry boat
and christen her *Sheila na Gig*.
She will open herself wide
to receive us in our automobiles,
two by two.

Our cars will be tied down,
blocked securely.
While we travel, her acolytes
wash and polish them,
vacuum interiors,
repair all problems.

Sheila na Gig will carry us
beyond the Ninth Wave,
beyond Tir-na-nOg, land
of perpetual youth.

On her wide sunlit upper deck,
we ladle soup
from her bronze cauldron,
dine on the roasted venison
hunters bring her in gratitude
for their luck,
eat the first fruits of the harvest,
dedicated to her.

We drink her sacred mead,
sing her sacred songs,
dance her sacred dances.

When we weary, we will find
a warm niche, lulled
as if nestled in a great water bed.
In our sleep, *Sheila* cleanses our minds
until they are as blank
as an unborn child's.
The images of our dreams
rise from our deep souls,
restoring our ancient heritage.

And when we wake,
Sheila na Gig will ferry us home,
opening herself as we drive off
in our shining, refurbished cars.
Returned,
we take up our lives again
with the new strength
that is her gift to us.
Sláinte, Síle!

THE GODDESS
WITHIN

You who want knowledge

HADEWIJCH II

You who want
knowledge,
seek the Oneness
within

There you
will find
the clear mirror
already waiting

from *Deep inside me at my core is where my mother lives*

CASSIA BERMAN

Deep inside me at my core
is where my Mother lives.
She is not in the noise of the world.
She is deep inside me.

The noise can talk about Her truth
but it is only in secret places in the body
that Her truth breathes.
Go into those places and transform
negative thoughts and feelings
into oneness with Her.

Let Her embrace you and be your friend.
She dwells deep in the heart of all matter
so to truly know Her is to have a friend everywhere
and everywhere be in Her embrace.
Let yourself relax now
and that secret embrace
will penetrate from inside outwards
dissolving your fears and anxieties and tensions
like the most profound massage.

I call my inner being Mother
for when She is released from within
She is like the Mother I loved
within the mother I knew —
larger and wiser, more loving and gentle
than the voice of the world in my mind,
which sometimes sounds like the mother I knew
but is losing its power to rule me.

Rosh Chodesh Tishrei

VICKI HOLLANDER

Ha-Borei,
You who create
You who breathe wind into my body,
once lifeless clay, now pulsing with life,
help me to do the labor of Tishrei
help me emerge
lustily into the world
with eyes wide open
hands   reaching
heart   pounding
lips   gasping   breath
soul as clear inside as a ray of sun
help me become anew

Ha-Borei,
You who create
give me strength for this Tishrei moon
to do the labor of birthing self
to walk the ways of spirit
to untwist the twisted
to wash the stained
to clear the clouded
to free my soul
just as the farmers in Tishrei
till their fields to receive the grains of winter
hoe the land to open to
submerged stalks of golden carrots
plush heads of purple beets
hold the increasing weight of the small

balls of curved leaves of cabbages and cauliflowers.
each year of our lives
we struggle, we work that more of us
may emerge

Ha–Borei
You who create
hold me as I struggle
to birth myself
I am red with blood
wrestling to come free
hard painful work to be born
twisting, turning, being pushed
wriggling to come out
from the warmth, from the shadows of what we know
to light, to air, to a new world
coming into my own
my birthright

There are many births
each resembles the first
and each is different
in each we struggle
to become more free
from that which binds us in
that we might become more of who our soul is
sing our unique song that only we can sing

To help us You have laid down
sacred days
like smooth white stones
more holy days now than in any other moon
for we need them
need them to midwife us to be born
anew
intricate stepping stones

that lead us over a
deep rushing stream
safely moored in earth
so pure you can see
the bottom
rocks all colors of gems
fish swimming
clear running waters

White stones
well carved by those who came before me
stones worn by others' feet
each hold me up
each bear me up
as I travel through the sacred days
their teachings feed the birthing self   •
milk we need suckle greedily
for it is life itself

So Ha-Borei,
cradle me, hold me
help me drink
let me rest in Your lap
and I will open gently
like the land gently receiving the first rains
like the fields abloom with daisies and meadow saffron
open and come again
into life

A Creed for Free Women*

Elsa Gidlow

I am.
I am from and of The Mother.
I am as I am.
Willfully harming none, none may question me.

As no free-growing tree serves another or requires to be served,
As no lion or lamb or mouse is bound or binds,
No plant or blade of grass nor ocean fish,
So I am not here to serve or be served.

I am Child of every Mother,
Mother of each daughter,
Sister of every woman,
And lover of whom I choose or chooses me.

Together or alone we dance Her Dance,
We do the work of The Mother,
She we have called Goddess for human comprehension,
She, the Source, never-to-be-grasped Mystery,
Terrible Cauldron, Womb,
Spinning out of her the unimaginably small
And the immeasurably vast—
Galaxies, worlds, flaming suns—
And our Earth, fertile with her beneficence,
Here, offering tenderest flowers.
(Yet flowers whose roots may split rock.)

I, we, Mothers, Sisters, Lovers,
Infinitely small out of her vastness,
Yet our roots too may split rock,
Rock of the rigid, the oppressive
In human affairs.

Thus is She
And being of Her
Thus am I.
Powered by Her,
As she gives, I may give,
Even of my blood and breath:
But none may require it;
And none may question me.

I am.
I am That I am.

*And such men as feel happy with it

Thou Gaia Art I

HEIDE GÖTTNER-ABENDROTH

the earth quivers wherever I go
in these zones of ripeness,
and sends out gentle visible waves—

through all things it vibrates in me,
wherever I happen to be
on the drifting floes—

you are the riddle under my feet
the depths in me, wherever I am
you are everywhere—

for Thou Gaia Art I

A Mermaid Knows

IRENE YOUNG

A mermaid dives deep.
She is not afraid of
what may be buried at the
bottom of her fluid heart.

She is not frozen in fear
watching from the dunes.
Instead a mermaid swims the waters
where she bathes in her own
self love.

To be a sea maid, one must breathe
with the wisdom that freedom
is not walking the shore, but
touching bottom with faith
that one rebounds to fresh waters,
through open eyes, with clear lungs,
a willing heart, and new skin
to breathe out the old,
and in the daring.

A mermaid knows
memory is both
a chain that binds,
and the key that frees;
And
the truth that heals
in the name of The Mother,
The Daughter, and The Holy Self.
Amen.

Watching the moon

Izumi Shikibu
translated by Jane Hirshfield with Mariko Aratani

Watching the moon
at dawn,
solitary, mid–sky,
I knew myself completely,
no part left out.

Apotheosis of the Kitchen Goddess II

TERESA NOELLE ROBERTS

There is a goddess and I know her. Her hands are not clean,
And she is large and strong and not too young. She wears
A sweatshirt with a hood and jeans, and sells black-purple
Eggplant, spinach, bright broccoli, sixty cents
The pound at the Greenmarket at Union Square. Her slat-side
    truck
Has Pennsylvania plates, and she says she lives near Lancaster.
But I know the truth, because her calloused hands turn earth
To things good to eat, and green, and lovely.

from *Imagine a Woman*

Patricia Lynn Reilly

Imagine a woman who honors the face of the Goddess
    in her own changing face,
A woman who celebrates the accumulation of her years
    and her wisdom.
Who refuses to use her precious life energy to
    disguise the changes in her body and life.

Imagine a woman who authors her own life,
A woman who exerts, initiates, and moves on her own behalf,
Who refuses to surrender except to her truest self,
    and to her wisest voice.

Imagine a woman who names her own gods,
A woman who imagines the divine in her own image and likeness,
Who designs her own spirituality
    and allows it to inform her daily life.

When a woman feels alone

MAY SARTON

"When a woman feels alone, when the room
Is full of daemons," the Nootka tribe
Tells us, "The Old Woman will be there."
She has come to me over three thousand miles
And what does she have to tell me, troubled
"by phantoms in the night"?
Is she really here?
What is the saving word from so deep in the past,
From as deep as the ancient root of the redwood,
From as deep as the primal bed of the ocean,
From as deep as a woman's heart sprung open
Again through a hard birth or a hard death?
Here under the shock of love, I am open
To you, Primal Spirit, one with rock and wave,
One with the survivors of flood and fire,
Who have rebuilt their homes a million times,
Who have lost their children and borne them again.
The words I hear are strength, laughter, endurance.
Old Woman I meet you deep inside myself.
There in the rootbed of fertility,
World without end, as the legend tells it.
Under the words you are my silence.

Song of the Self: The Grandmother

ALMA LUZ VILLANUEVA

Surrounded by my shields, am
I:
Surrounded by my children, am
I:
Surrounded by the void, am
I:
I am the void.
I am the womb of remembrance.
I am the flowering darkness.
I am the flower, first flesh.

Utter darkness I inhabit—
There, I watch creation unfold—
There I know we begin and end—
Only to begin, again and again—
Again. In this darkness, I am
Turning, turning toward a birth:
My own—a newborn grandmother
Am I, suckling light. Rainbow
Serpent covers me, head to foot,
In endless circles—covers me,
That I may live forever, in this
Form or another. The skin she
Leaves behind glitters with
The question, with the answer,
With the promise:
"Do you remember yourself?"
"I am always woman."
"Flesh is flower, forever."

I enter darkness to enter birth,
To wear the Rainbow, to hear her
Hissing loudly, clearly, in my
Inner ear: love.

I am spiraling. I am spinning.
I am singing this Grandmother's Song.
I am remembering forever, where we
Belong.

Corn Children

CAROL LEE SANCHEZ

we gather our bones from many places, look for
familiar marks to determine our identities.
we share the land marks. places. buildings.
local folks.   seen with different eyes:
simon,   leslie,   paula,   and i.

i speak mostly of earth with brush and paint.
desert.   mesa.   hill and mountain.   rock.
sagebrush.   yucca and cedar.   thunders
and cloud people.

                                   earth colors
                                   sky colors
hand and eye proclaim on canvas and paper these
visions in my head.   in my heart.

with my brush i describe earth mother—
to remind my children the land is sacred.
this sacred altar that holds the length of one
star's breath.

with my pen i speak of relationships
with words and the ordering of them, tell little
stories.   keep hold of that harmony i am
part of.   that order of things reflected in being
                                   and spirit.

it seems proper that language should reflect harmony:
                               a giving way
                               a moving out
                               a coming in.

these things we speak about from memory
as corn children,
these traditions we keep not knowing why sometimes
or how we know the right ways.

many corn grandmothers watch over us
and whisper into the wind to remind us of our duties:

> you should never take more than you need.
> if you need some reeds for the new whisk broom
> then you go down to the river and tell the spirits
> all around you there, that you
> have come for some reeds.
> you must ask them for permission and
> then you must thank them for providing
> for you.

in this way, we keep in balance.   in this way we keep
in harmony. we should always be courteous to
everything—that's what grandma used to say.

bones of thoughts are in those burial mounds or are
around them. sometimes they are disturbed when the
mounds are plundered but those thoughts remain
for us if we respect our ancestors.
thoughts that come to tell us:

> > that's the way it is
> > that's the way it is to be done.

HER WORDS

from *The Thunder: Perfect Mind*

GNOSTIC GOSPEL

NAG HAMMADI LIBRARY, 200–300 CE

Look upon me,
you who meditate,
and hearers, hear.
Whoever is waiting for me,
take me into yourselves.
Do not drive me
out of your eyes,
or out of your voice,
or out of your ears.
Observe. Do not forget who I am.

For I am the first, and the last.
I am the honored one, and the scorned.
I am the whore and the holy one.
I am the wife and the virgin.
I am the mother, the daughter,
and every part of both.
I am the barren one who has borne many sons.
I am she whose wedding is great
and I have not accepted a husband.
I am the midwife and the childless one,
the easing of my own labor.
I am the bride and the bridegroom
and my husband is my father.
I am the mother of my father,
the sister of my husband;
my husband is my child.
My offspring are my own birth,

the source of my power,
what happens to me is their wish.

I am the incomprehensible silence
and the memory that will not be forgotten.
I am the voice whose sound is everywhere
and the speech that appears in many forms.
I am the utterance of my own name.

. . . I am knowledge and ignorance.
I am modesty and boldness.
I am shameless, I am ashamed.
I am strength and I am fear.
I am war and I am peace.

. . . I am the one they call Life,
the one you call Death.
I am the one they call Law,
the one you call Lawless.
I am the one you have scattered,
and you have gathered me together.

. . . I am the joining and the dissolving.
I am what lasts, and what goes.
I am the one going down,
and the one toward whom they ascend.
I am the condemnation and the acquittal.
For myself, I am sinless,
and the roots of sin grow in my being.
I am the desire of the outer,
and control of the inner.
I am the hearing in everyone's ears,
I am the speech which cannot be heard.
I am the mute who is speechless,
great are the multitudes of my words.

On reading the new physics—
Creation & Cosmology

COSI FABIAN

I am space
I am the stars

Each element
present in that
first iota of time
Is in me

All time
has expanded
To this moment

All creation
flows
In my blood

Exploding novas
flash
In my eyes

My breath
is the rush
Of suns

I am space
I am the stars

Briefly It Enters, and Briefly Speaks

JANE KENYON

I am the blossom pressed in a book,
found again after two hundred years. . . .

I am the maker, the lover, and the keeper. . . .

When the young girl who starves
sits down to a table
she will sit beside me. . . .

I am food on the prisoner's plate. . . .

I am water rushing to the wellhead,
filling the pitcher until it spills. . . .

I am the patient gardener
of the dry and weedy garden. . . .

I am the stone step,
the latch, and the working hinge. . . .

I am the heart contracted by joy . . .
the longest hair, white
before the rest. . . .

I am there in the basket of fruit
presented to the widow. . . .

I am the musk rose opening
unattended, the fern on the boggy summit. . . .

I am the one whose love
overcomes you, already with you
when you think to call my name. . . .

Behold This and Always Love It

MERIDEL LE SUEUR

O my daughters
My bowl is full of sweet grass,
I approach in my best buckskin,
I travel the path of the people
Behold me!
The white buffalo woman brings the
        sacred pipe of vision.
Standing on the hill behold me
        Coming coming coming
Over the prairie breast I come
        sacred,
Covered by a cloud of flowers.
Behold what you see, my grandchildren
        Behold this
And always love it.

She moves   she moves   all moves to her.
In the bowl   the basket   the earth bowl
She is adorned in the middle country
she appears in the crops of Kansas.
In Oklahoma brothels,
In erupting volcanoes,
At the peyote ceremony of birds.
In the hell holes and the heavenly meadows
    she appears.
From far away she is coming   coming.
From all the roads she is coming   coming.
They are gathering.   They are coming.

from *Homecoming*

LINDA REUTHER

And the Great Mother said:

Come my child and give me all that you are.
I am not afraid of your strength and darkness, of your fear and
 pain.
Give me your tears. They will be my rushing rivers and roaring
 oceans.
Give me your rage. It will erupt into my molten volcanoes and
 rolling thunder.
Give me your tired spirit. I will lay it to rest in my soft meadows.
Give me your hopes and dreams. I will plant a field of sunflowers
 and arch
rainbows in the sky.
You are not too much for me. My arms and heart welcome your
 true fullness.
There is room in my world for all of you, all that you are.
I will cradle you in the boughs of my ancient redwoods and the
 valleys of my
gentle rolling hills.
My soft winds will sing you lullabies and soothe your burdened
 heart.
Release your deep pain. You are not alone and you have never
 been alone. . . .

The Goddesses

JANINE CANAN

Every being is immortal, says the first Goddess.
May the demons not crouch on your chest, says the second.
The eyes of the third Goddess well with tenderness.
The fourth is radiant with young life.
Very hard, utters the fifth.
More work to be done—says the sixth, *first sit in the sun.*
The seventh delights, *Is your heart shattering?*
The eighth bursts with righteous indignation.
The ninth will not judge.
The tenth Goddess calls, *I will come!*
The eleventh sighs, *There is nothing to be done.*
Beyond this pain, coos the twelfth, *are treasures.*
Everything, proclaims the thirteenth Goddess,
is perfect as it is.

from *The Network of the Imaginary Mother*

ROBIN MORGAN

As it was in the beginning,
    I say:
    Here is your sacrament—

        Take. Eat. This is my body,
        this real milk, thin, sweet, bluish,
        which I give for the life of the world.
        Like sap to spring it rises
        even before the first faint cry is heard,
        an honest nourishment
        alone able to sustain you.

    I say:
    Here is your eternal testament—

        This cup, this chalice, this primordial cauldron
        of real menstrual blood
        the color of clay warm with promise,
        rhythmic, cyclical, fit for lining the uterus
        and shed for many,
        for the remission of living.

    Here is your bread of life.
    Here is the blood by which you live in me.

The World Disc, The Great Round,
The Wheel of Transformation.
Two solstices, summer and winter.
Two equinoxes, spring and fall.

One day to stand outside the year, unutterable.
Thirteen-fold is my lunar calendar,
Five-fold my mysteries, my kiss,
Three-fold my face.

And this is the secret, once unquestioned,
     - sought in the oldest trances of us all:
the large male children forced into exile
from their pelvic cradle, wailing, refusing to leave;
the grown female children, knotting together the skein
of generations, each loop in the coil a way back
to that heart of memory we cannot escape,
yet long for still.

No more need you dream this, my children,
in remembrance of me.
There is a place beyond your struggle
where I will take us.
It will exist, see, I am creating it now.
I have said so.

Blessed be my brain
    that I may conceive of my own power.
Blessed be my breast
    that I may give sustenance to those I love.
Blessed be my womb
    that I may create what I choose to create.
Blessed be my knees
    that I may bend so as not to break.
Blessed be my feet
    that I may walk in the path of my highest will.

Now is the seal of my vision
set upon my flesh.

You call me by a thousand names, uttering yourselves.

Earthquake I answer you, flood and volcano flow—
    the Warning.
    This to remind you that I am the Old One
    who holds the Key, the Crone to whom all things return.

Lotus I answer you, lily, corn-poppy, centripetal rose—
    the Choice.
    This is to remind you that I am the Mother
    who unravels from herself the net sustaining you.

Moon I answer you, my gibbous eye, the regenerating carapace,
    the Milky Way—
    the Possibility.
    This to remind you that I am the Virgin
    born only now, new, capable of all invention.

I have been with you from the beginning,
utterly simple.
I will be with you when you die,
say what you will.
We shall never be finished.
This is possible,
a small gift, hush.

There is nothing I have not been,
and I am come into my power.

There is nothing I cannot be.

ABOUT THE CONTRIBUTORS

PAULA GUNN ALLEN has published numerous works of poetry, fiction, and essays that center on women, spirituality, and Indian country. Her most recent poetry collection, *Life Is a Fatal Disease,* and essay collection, *Off the Reservation: Reflections on Boundary-Busting, Border-Crossing Loose Canons,* offer a variety of views on the interconnections among these three. She recently retired from the English department at UCLA. Ms. Allen can be reached at www.sulis-sophia.org.

JUDITH ANDERSON is a printmaker in Miller Place, New York. Her etchings have been published in Elinor W. Gadon's *The Once and Future Goddess,* Burleigh Mutén's *Return of the Great Goddess,* Mary R. Hopkins's videos *Woman and Her Symbols,* and Bill Moyers's PBS program (and video) *Spirit and Nature.*

LUCIUS APULEIUS (2nd century) was a priest and storyteller whose classic, *The Golden Ass,* includes one of the oldest written versions of the tale of Psyche and Cupid, which appears in the context of an adventure that culminates in the worship of Isis.

ANNE BARING is the author of *The One Work: A Journey toward the Self,* and is coauthor with Jules Cashford of *The Myth of the Goddess* and with Andrew Harvey of *The Mystic Vision* and *The Divine Feminine.*

SUZANNE BENTON is an artist working in multiple media. She performs her narrative poetry with metal sculptured masks that she has also created. A transculturalist, her venues stretch beyond New York City's art world to villages in Africa, India, and Nepal, and to philosophy and education portals from Calcutta to Cambridge. Honors include numerous artist-in-residences and grants worldwide.

JENNIFER BEREZAN is a singer/songwriter whose healing recordings include *In the Eye of the Storm, Borderlines, She Carries Me,* and *Refuge.* She performs and teaches music and healing internationally and leads women's pilgrimages to sacred goddess sites. She is currently working on her new project, *Returning,* to be recorded in the Hypogeum in Malta.

CASSIA BERMAN is a poet (*Divine Mother Within Me*), writer, and editor whose poems and articles about the intersection of spirituality and daily life have been published in magazines and anthologies—including *Yoga Journal, American Poetry Review, Species Link, Mother of the Universe, Divine Mosaic*. She lives in Woodstock, New York, where she teaches t'ai chi, qi gong, and workshops in poetry and women's spirituality.

JALAJA BONHEIM is a counselor and internationally known workshop leader who was raised in Europe and studied Indian temple dance in India. Her books include *Aphrodite's Daughters: Women's Sexual Stories and the Journey of the Soul* and *Goddess: A Celebration in Art and Literature*. She is currently working on a new book called *The Hunger for Ecstasy*.

Z BUDAPEST is an internationally acclaimed teacher of women's spirituality and the author of six books, including *The Holy Book of Women's Mysteries, Grandmother Moon, The Grandmother of Time, Goddess in the Office, Goddess in the Bedroom*, and *Summoning the Fates*. She emigrated to the United States from Hungary in 1956 and is one of the founders of the contemporary goddess movement in the United States. She has organized numerous conferences and festivals celebrating the Goddess, and is the director of the Women's Spirituality Forum, P.O. Box 11363, Oakland, CA 94611. Ms. Budapest can be reached at 1-900-737-4637 for mentoring readings.

JANINE CANAN is a psychiatrist who resides in Sonoma, California. She is the author of ten books of poetry, including the award-winning anthology *She Rises Like the Sun;* a new chapbook, *Love, Enter,* selected from her forthcoming *Changing Woman;* and her translations of Else Lasker-Schueler, *Star in My Forehead*.

CHAROULA, a native of Greece, translates poetry, fiction, and essays from ancient and modern Greek into English. She is an artist, an importer of goddess statues, an herbalist, and a polarity therapy practitioner. She leads women's journeys to sacred Greek sites. She resides in Greece and in the United States.

LUCILLE CLIFTON was born in Depew, New York in 1936. She is the author of *Good Times, Good News about the Earth; An Ordinary Woman; Two-Headed Woman; Good Woman: Poems and a Memoir 1969–1980; Next: New Poems; Quilting: Poems 1987–1990;* and *The Book of Light*. Her awards include two nominations for the Pulitzer Prize in poetry, an Emmy

Award from the American Academy of Television Arts and Sciences, and two fellowships from the National Endowment for the Arts.

JONATHAN COTT is the author of thirteen books, including *The Search for Omm Sety; Pipers at the Gates of Dawn: The Wisdom of Children's Literature;* two volumes of interviews (*Forever Young* and *Visions and Voices*); *Wandering Ghost: The Odyssey of Lafcadio Hearn; Isis and Osiris;* and two volumes of poetry (*City of Earthly Love* and *Charms*). He lives in New York City.

CHANI DIPRIMA is a twenty-year-old native San Franciscan who began writing in earnest when she was fifteen. She published her first book of poetry in 1996. Ms. DiPrima studied writing at Naropa and with her grandmother, Diane di Prima. She is working on her second book of poetry. She lives with her mother and brother in Oakland, California.

DIANE DI PRIMA is the author of more than thirty books of poetry and prose, which have been translated into thirteen languages. Born in New York in the 1930s, she was active in the Beat movement. She moved to the West Coast in 1968 and currently lives in San Francisco, where she works as a writer, teacher, and healer and studies alchemy and Tibetan Buddhism. Her most recent books are *Pieces of a Song: Selected Poems* and *Loba*. The first volume of her autobiography, *Recollections of My Life as a Woman,* will be published in the year 2000.

ECLIPSE is an activist, healer, ritual artist, priestess, visionary, and author of *The Moon in Hand*. Deeply involved in the empowerment of women and the return of the ancient religions, Eclipse cofounded Earth Calls Network, an ecofeminist organization dedicated to preserving the living body and spirit of Earth. A codirector of WomenCircles for fourteen years, she is working on three books and a film script and advocating for elephants in captivity. Eclipse resides in Rhode Island.

ENHEDUANNA (ca. 2300 BCE) was a Sumerian priestess who was herself worshipped as a personification of the goddess Inanna. Several of her hymns in praise of Inanna have been translated for the first time during this century from the cuneiform.

COSI FABIAN is a poet, teacher, performer, and political activist. Born on the island of Malta and raised in England, she lives in San Francisco. Her twenty-year dedication to the goddess Inanna, She-of-the-Wondrous-Vulva, called her to become a "sacred prostitute" in the real world at the age of forty-two. Her essay on this subject appears in *Whores and Other Feminists*. Ms. Fabian can be reached at Cosi@Sirius.com.

ELSA GIDLOW (1898–1986) wrote the first North American poetry book to celebrate lesbian love, *On a Grey Thread* (1923), as well as the first full-life explicitly lesbian autobiography, *Elsa, I Come with My Song* (1986). Ms. Gidlow triumphed over poverty, lack of formal education, and family tragedy to create a large body of work and to found Druid Heights, a Taoist-inspired retreat in the California redwoods. A devout progressive, she was indicted by McCarthy in the 1950s, and as always boldly championed free thought over dogmatism.

SHEILAH GLOVER is a jazz/cabaret performer with the award-winning trio Nicholas, Glover, and Wray. She is also a music programmer for Pacifica station KPFA and the producer of projects and CDs for other artists. In 1994 she released a CD of her own songs, *Power of the Soul*. She recently adopted a daughter from an orphanage in China.

STARR GOODE is a writer and lecturer who lives in Santa Monica, California. She is currently working on a book on Sheila na Gig. She is a member of the coven Nemesis.

LYNN GOTTLIEB was one of the first women to be ordained as a rabbi. She is well known for her efforts to fuse feminism, mysticism, craft, and social action with traditional Jewish teaching to create a contemporary Judaism. She cofounded Congregation Nahalat Shalom in Albuquerque, New Mexico. She is the author of *She Who Dwells Within*.

HEIDE GÖTTNER-ABENDROTH, Ph.D., is the author of *The Goddess and Her Heros: Matriarchal Religion in Mythology, Fairy Tales, and Poetry* and *The Dancing Goddess: Principles of a Matriarchal Aesthetic*. In 1986 she founded the women's academy HAGIA, Academy for Research on Matriarchy, in the Bavarian Forest, where she is director. In 1993, she received a scholarship from the University of Bremen for her research on matriarchy.

JUDY GRAHN is an internationally known woman-centered poet and cultural theorist. She has published numerous books of poetry and a gay and lesbian cultural history, *Another Mother Tongue*, which have won awards. Her latest book, *Blood, Bread, and Roses: How Menstruation Created the World*, contains a theory of culture and consciousness. Ms. Grahn is working on a Ph.D. in women's spirituality and teaches her own work in San Francisco at New College of California in the Women's Spirituality M.A. and the Writing and Consciousness M.A. Programs. See www.Serpentina.com.

SUSAN GRIFFIN is a feminist writer, poet, essayist, lecturer, teacher, playwright, and filmmaker. She is the author of more than twenty books, including *A Chorus of Stones: The Private Life of War; The Eros of Everyday Life: Essays on Ecology, Gender, and Society; Woman and Nature;* and *Pornography and Silence,* as well as several collections of poetry, including *Like the Iris of an Eye, Unremembered Country,* and *Bending Home.* She lives in the hills of Berkeley, California.

H.D. (Hilda Doolittle, 1886–1961) published her first book of poems, *Sea Garden,* internationally in 1916. At that time she was part of a London group of writers known as the Imagists, which included D. H. Lawrence and Ezra Pound. H. D. traveled abroad extensively and was involved with early filmmaking in Germany as a scriptwriter and an actress, in addition to being a prolific poet. Her books include *Trilogy, Helen in Egypt, Tribute to the Angels, The Flowering of the Rod, End to Torment: A Memoir of Pound, By Avon River,* and *Bid Me to Live.*

HADEWIJCH (13th century) was a Flemish Beguine mystic whose body of work is based on the concept of divine love. She wrote *Poems in Stanzas, Poems in Couplets,* and *Letters,* as well as a collection entitled *Visions.*

ANDREW HARVEY is the author of *Journey to Ladakh, Hidden Journey, The Way of Passion: A Celebration of Rumi,* and is a coauthor with Mark Matousek of *Dialogues with a Modern Mystic* and with Anne Baring of *The Mystic Vision* and *The Divine Feminine.*

ZIPORAH HILDEBRANDT is the author of several short science fiction stories and children's books, including *This Is Our Seder,* as well as articles and a book on flower essences. She works as an astrologer and flower essence therapist in western Massachusetts. A graduate of Hampshire College, she is married and the mother of a homeschooled daughter.

HILDEGARD OF BINGEN (1098–1179) was a visionary Benedictine nun and abbess, as well as a poet, composer, healer, and theologian. Her best known works are the *Scivias,* which records many of her visions, and the *Symphonia,* a cycle of over seventy liturgical songs.

PRISCILLA BAIRD HINCKLEY is an artist and teacher who has lived and worked on three continents seeking insights into how expressive actions (including the arts) communicate ideas that shape societies. She lectured on African art at Tufts University for several years.

JANE HIRSHFIELD is an author, editor, and translator who has received a Guggenheim Fellowship and other awards for her poetry. Her collections of poetry include *Of Gravity and Angels, Alaya,* and *The October Palace.* She is the editor and translator of *The Ink Dark Moon* and *Women in Praise of the Sacred.* She lives in northern California.

LEX HIXON (1942–1995) was a teacher and writer who was spiritually initiated in five traditions—Ramakrishna Vedanta, Eastern Orthodox Christianity, Helveti-Jerrahi Sufism, Zen, and Tibetan Buddhism. He was well known as the host of *In the Spirit,* a radio program on which he interviewed some of the world's foremost spiritual leaders. He authored seven books, including *Mother of the Universe: Visions of the Goddess and Tantric Hymns of Enlightenment, Great Swan: Meetings with Ramakrishna,* and the classic *Coming Home: The Experience of Enlightenment in Sacred Traditions.*

VICKI HOLLANDER is a rabbi, a marriage and family therapist, a former hospice bereavement coordinator, and a writer of rituals and poetry. She lives in Vancouver, British Columbia, where her private practice focuses on grief and loss issues, bereavement, and life transitions. She offers classes, workshops, and retreats on women and spirituality, grief, and conscious living–conscious dying.

HOMER (8th century BCE) was a Greek epic poet, the reputed author of the *Iliad* and the *Odyssey* as well as a series of hymns about many of the Olympian deities.

INGE HOOGERHUIS is a professional singer. Born in Holland to a Jewish atheist mother and a Protestant father, her spiritual searching has been centered around finding her own true voice. Writing has always been an integral part of the journey.

SUZANNE IRONBITER has a doctorate in the history of religion from Columbia University and teaches at SUNY Purchase College. She is the author of *Devi,* a book-length narrative poem expanding on stories of the Indian goddess of war, wisdom, and love and on other mythological poems from various cultures.

IZUMI SHIKIBU (970–1030) served as a court poet in the Japanese Heian court of Empress Akiko. She is considered the most outstanding woman poet of Japanese literature.

BABA IFA KARADE is the author of *The Handbook of Yoruba Religious Concepts* and a priest of Obatala and high priest of Orunmila, having been initiated into the mysteries of Yoruba culture in Nigeria. He teaches junior high and career development in New Jersey.

MIM KELBER is a feminist author and activist and was a longtime policy adviser and speechwriter for the late Bella Abzug. Together they founded Women USA Fund, the Women's Foreign Policy Council, and, in 1990, the Women's Environment and Development Organization. WEDO is an international network of women working together for a peaceful, healing planet with equal participation of women and men in decision making. Ms. Kelber lives in Brooklyn Heights with her husband. She is the mother of two daughters and five grandchildren.

JANE KENYON (1947–1995) was the author of five collections of poetry (*Otherwise, From Room to Room, The Boat of Quiet Hours, Let Evening Come,* and *Constance*) and the translator of *Twenty Poems of Anna Akhmatova.* She was awarded a Guggenheim Fellowship and the PEN Voelcker Award, and was featured with her husband, Donald Hall, in the Emmy Award–winning Bill Moyers special *A Life Together.*

ELANA KLUGMAN is a writer and psychotherapist living in Shutesbury, Massachusetts, with her husband and children. She has published poems in *Our Bodies, Ourselves; Mothering* magazine; and *Which Lilith.*

SARA KLUGMAN is a six-year-old living in Shutesbury, Massachusetts, with her parents and her brother. She composed *God's Body* when she was four while walking in the woods with her mother. Fortunately, her mother had pen and paper to record the poem as it was spoken. Sara loves mice, dancing, playing piano, and writing poems.

LEAH KORICAN is a poet and visual artist. Her work has been published in a number of chapbooks, *Lunacycle, Her Story,* and the forthcoming *Kitchen Songs,* as well as in *Return of the Great Goddess.* Her visual art has been shown nationally and is included in numerous private collections. She lives in Oakland, California, with her husband and son and teaches at the Bentley School.

PEM KREMER is a poet and assistant professor at the University of Kentucky, where she teaches in the Honors Humanities Program and in the English department. Her work has appeared in *Cries of the Spirit* and *Return of the Great Goddess.*

MARILYN KRYSL is the author of seven books of poetry and three short-story collections. She taught English in China, worked as a volunteer for the human rights organization Peace Brigade International in Sri Lanka, and worked at Mother Teresa's Sisters of Charity in Calcutta. She is director of the Creative Writing Program at the University of Colorado in Boulder. Her latest book of stories is *How to Accommodate Men* (1998).

LAO-TZU (6th century BCE) was the keeper of the imperial archives and a contemporary of Confucius. He reputedly recorded his teachings in the classic text of Taoism, the *Tao-te Ching*.

MERIDEL LE SUEUR (1900–1996) published five books of poetry, including *Rites of Ancient Ripening*, and twelve books of prose, including *Harvest and Song for My Times, 1919–1945; The Girl; Worker Writers: I Hear Men Talking; Women on the Bread Lines; Ripening;* and *North Star Country*.

JOAN SLESINGER LOGGHE is the winner of a National Endowment for the Arts Fellowship in poetry, and for seven years was poetry editor for *Mothering* magazine. Her books include *What Makes a Woman Beautiful, Twenty Years in Bed with the Same Man, Sofia,* and *Blessed Resistance*. She lives in La Puebla, New Mexico.

BOBBY MCFERRIN is one of the world's most innovative, virtuosic, and entertaining performing artists. He is recognized as a singer, orchestrator, and conductor. He dedicated "The 23rd Psalm" from his CD *Medicine Music* to his mother.

JANE MCVEIGH is the author of *With a Poet's Eye: Children Translate the World*. She teaches fifth grade at the Abington Friend's School outside Philadelphia. Her work has appeared in *Cream City Review, Iris,* and *Beloit Poetry Journal*.

BETTY DE SHONG MEADOR is a Jungian analyst in Berkeley, California, and a past president of the C. G. Jung Institute of San Francisco. Her translations of the Sumerian poetry of the goddess Inanna appear in her book *Uncursing the Dark*, and her translations of the poems of the high priestess Enheduanna are forthcoming in *Inanna: Lady of Largest Heart*.

PATRICIA MONAGHAN is the author of *The New Book of Goddesses and Heroines*, an encyclopedia of the world's feminine divinities; *O Mother Sun: A New View of the Cosmic Feminine;* and *Magical Gardens*. She is also the author of two books of poetry: *Winterburning* and *Seasons of the Witch*.

A lifelong Alaskan, she now resides in Chicago, where she teaches inter-disciplinary studies at DePaul University.

ROBIN MORGAN is an award-winning poet, novelist, political theorist, feminist activist, journalist, and editor. She has published fourteen books, including five of poetry, two of fiction, and the now-classic anthologies *Sisterhood Is Powerful* and *Sisterhood Is*. A founder and leader of contemporary U.S. feminism, she has also been active in the international women's movement for more than two decades. Her books include *Upstairs in the Garden: Poems Selected and New, The Word of a Woman: Feminist Dispatches,* and *The Anatomy of Freedom: Feminism in Four Dimensions*. She lives in New York City.

BURLEIGH MUTÉN is the author of two children's books, *Grandmother's Stories: Wise Woman Tales from Around the World* and *Great Goddesses of the World*. She is founder of Hands of the Goddess Press, which originally published her *Return of the Goddess* engagement calendar. She is also the author and editor of *Return of the Great Goddess*. She is the mother of two children.

KATHLEEN NORRIS is the author of *Cloister Walk, Little Girls in Church, Dakota, Falling Off,* and *The Middle of the World* as well as several chapbooks. Her work has appeared in many journals, including the *Chicago Review,* the *Nation,* and the *New Yorker*. She is a reviewer for the *New York Times* and the *American Book Review*. She lives in South Dakota.

YOKO ONO is a multimedia artist who constantly challenges and stretches the traditional boundaries of sculpture, painting, film, photography, theater, and music. She helped found the Fluxus art movement in the early 1960s and is the author of *Grapefruit* and *Instruction Paintings* and the subject of numerous web pages including such interactive web events as "Yoko Ono, One Woman Show" (hosted by the Museum of Contemporary Art, Los Angeles) and "Acorns, One Hundred Days With Yoko Ono." Eight of her solo albums, as well as four albums with John Lennon and the Plastic Ono Band, are available from Rykodisc. Her most recent album, *Rising,* is available from Capitol Records.

PAT PARNELL is a poet, journalist, and educator whose work has appeared in *Re-Imaging,* the *New Hampshire College Journal, Voices from the Center, Touchstone,* and *Return of the Goddess 1999*. She is Professor Emerita of Communications and Media at White Pines College, Chester, New Hampshire, where she teaches courses in feminist theology and women's spirituality, and coeditor of *Compass Rose*, the White Pines literary and art journal.

PATRICIA LYNN REILLY holds a master of divinity degree from Princeton Theological Seminary and postgraduate certification from the Women's Theological Center in women's spirituality and feminist theology. She is the founder of Open Window Creations, where she conducts workshops and retreats on women's spirituality, recovery, and the healing ministry. She is also codirector of the Circle of Life Women's Center. She lives in Berkeley, California.

PATRICIA REIS is a writer, teacher, and psychotherapist. She is the author of *Through the Goddess: A Women's Way of Healing, Daughters of Saturn: From Father's Daughter to Creative Woman,* and, with Susan Amons, *The Dreaming Way: Art and Dreams for Remembering and Recovery.* She lives in Maine.

LINDA REUTHER has created a healing retreat center, Hearts and Hands at Cider Creek, on the northern California coast in Albion, California. Her vision and purpose is to create a nurturing environment where people can reconnect to the sacred feminine in themselves, each other, and Mother Earth on the path to their own wholeness.

JOYCE RUPP is a member of the Servants of Mary community, a freelance writer, and a retreat director. She is the author of *Fresh Bread, Praying Our Goodbyes,* and *The Star in My Heart.* She lives in Des Moines, Iowa.

CAROL LEE SANCHEZ is a poet and teacher, recently honored as writer of the year by Wordcraft Circle of Native Writers and Storytellers. Her most recent book of poetry is *From Spirit to Matter.* A native New Mexican of Laguna Pueblo and Lebanese heritage, she currently lives on a farm in Missouri.

SAPPHO (7th–6th century BCE), a renowned poet of her era, founded a girls school on the island of Lesbos, Greece, where the practice of honoring Aphrodite and the Muses was cultivated.

MAY SARTON (1912–1995) was an acclaimed poet, novelist, and writer of journals. Her novels include *Mrs. Stevens Hears the Mermaids Singing, The Education of Harriet Hatfield,* and *The Magnificent Spinster.* Ms. Sarton's most recent work includes *Collected Poems, 1930–1993* and *Coming into Eighty.* Thirty-eight of her works are currently in print.

NTOZAKE SHANGE is the author of the Obie Award–winning *For Colored Girls Who Have Considered Suicide/When the Rainbow is Enuf*. She has written numerous novels, books of poetry, and plays. Ms. Shange is associate professor of drama and English at Prairie View A&M University in Texas. She has received a National Endowment for the Arts Fellowship and a Guggenheim Fellowship in addition to several other awards of recognition.

LESLIE SIMON is the author of several books of poetry, including *High Desire, Collisions and Transformations,* and, with Jan Johnson Drantell, *A Music I No Longer Heard: The Early Death of a Parent*. She teaches women's studies at City College of San Francisco. She lives in San Francisco, where she raised her daughter and son.

JUDITH SORNBERGER is the author of *Open Heart* and two chapbooks, *Judith Beheading Holofernes* and *Bifocals Barbie: A Midlife Pantheon*. She is in the final stages of revising *Wild Season: A Midlife Reckoning,* a chapter of which appeared in the fall 1998 issue of *Prairie Schooner*. She lives in Pennsylvania.

STARHAWK is a writer, teacher, counselor, political activist, nonviolence trainer, and witch. She is a founding member of Reclaiming: A Center for Feminist Spirituality and Counseling in San Francisco. Starhawk is the author of *The Spiral Dance: A Rebirth of the Ancient Religion of the Great Goddess, Dreaming the Dark, The Fifth Sacred Thing, Walking to Mercury,* and, with Diane Baker and Anne Hill, *Circle Round: Raising Children in Goddess Traditions*.

GENEVIEVE TAGGARD (1894–1948) authored eleven books of poetry, including *For Eager Lovers* and *Slow Music*. She taught literature at three colleges and edited four anthologies of poetry and two literary magazines, one of which she founded. She wrote dozens of book reviews, many articles, some short stories, and a biography, *The Life and Mind of Emily Dickinson*. A collection of her work, anthologized by her daughter, Marcia D. Liles, is entitled *To the Natural World*.

GABRIELE UHLEIN, O.S.F., Ph.D., is a Wheaton Franciscan sister and a member of the Franciscan Federation Spirit and Life Committee. She is the author of *Meditations with Hildegard of Bingen* and is pioneering the Franciscan Center for Incarnation Studies. She offers workshops and retreats on rediscovering the holy in the ordinary and the divine at work in every event of life.

DOREEN VALIENTE is the author of *Witchcraft for Tomorrow, Natural Magic,* and *An ABC of Witchcraft, Past and Present.* She resides in the United Kingdom.

ALMA LUZ VILLANUEVA is the author of several award-winning books, including *The Ultraviolet Sky, Naked Ladies, Planet, Weeping Woman, La Llorona and Other Stories,* and *Desire,* which was nominated for a Pulitzer Prize 1998. Her work has appeared in *Ms.* magazine as well as many other publications and anthologies. She is the mother of four grown children and two grandchildren.

MIRIAM THERESE WINTER is professor of liturgy, worship, and spirituality at Hartford Seminary, Hartford, Connecticut. She has recorded a dozen music albums, including the award-winning *Joy Is Like the Rain,* and is author of several award-winning books, including *WomanWord, WomanWisdom, WomanWitness,* and *The Gospel According to Mary.*

DIANE WOLKSTEIN is the author of twenty books, including *The Magic Orange Tree* and *Inanna, Queen of Heaven and Earth.* She has performed and collected stories on five continents. Ms. Wolkstein teaches mythology at New York University and gives workshops on storytelling worldwide.

IRENE YOUNG is a freelance photographer/writer internationally known for her portraits of musicians and authors. She has more than four hundred CD covers to her credit. Her spiritual art has been featured in books such as *Return of the Great Goddess.* She sees photography and poetry as sisters, since, prior to conception, timing and imagery dance together.

CREDITS

Every effort has been made to trace copyright holders of material in this book. The editor apologizes if any work has been used without permission and would be glad to be told of anyone who has not been consulted.

Allen, Paula Gunn. "He Na Tye Woman" from *Shadow Country*. © 1982 by The Regents of the University of California. By permission of the author.

Anderson, Judith. "Re-member Us." © 1990 by Judith Anderson. By permission of the author.

Anonymous. "Holy Goddess Tellus" from *Goddess: Mother of Living Nature*. Adele Getty. Thames & Hudson © 1990.

Anonymous. "Hymn to Ishtar" from *The Seven Tablets of Creation*. L. W. King, London, 1902.

Anonymous. "Litany to Our Lady" from *Ireland's Women: Writings Past and Present,* ed. K. Donovan, A. Jeffares, and B. Kennelly. © 1994. W. W. Norton.

Apuleius, Lucius. "I Am Nature, Mother of All" from *The Golden Ass*. H. G. Bohn, London, 1853.

Baring, Anne. "The Song" from *The Divine Feminine,* by Andrew Harvey and Anne Baring. Godsfield Press, U.K., 1996.

Benton, Suzanne. "Lilith" and "The Second Coming" © 1971 and 1979, respectively, by Suzanne Benton. To commemorate her NYC Mask and Ritual Procession: Celebrating the Second Coming of the Great Goddess. By permission of the author.

Berezan, Jennifer. "Hail Mother" from the recording *She Carries Me*. © 1995 by Jennifer Berezan. Edge of Wonder Records, P.O. Box 6181, Albany, CA 94706. E-mail: Berezan@sirius.com. By permission of the author.

Berman, Cassia. Excerpt from "Deep inside me at my core is where my mother lives," "Poem for the Shechina," and "Mother Lakshmi's Poem" from *Divine Mother Within Me*. © 1995 by Cassia Berman, Divine Mother Communications, Woodstock, N.Y. By permission of the author.

Bonheim, Jalaja, ed. "Tantric Praise of the Goddess" and "Homage to

Glover, Sheilah. "Power of the Soul" © 1998 by Sheilah Glover. Reprinted by permission of the author.

Goode, Starr. "Lady of Pazardzik" © 1989 by Starr Goode. By permission of the author.

Gottlieb, Lynn. "Greeting Shekinah" and "A Meditation on the Feminine Nature of Shekinah" © 1995 by Lynn Gottlieb. Reprinted by permission of HarperCollins Publishers.

Göttner-Abendroth, Heide. "Thou Gaia Art I" © 1992 by Heide Göttner-Abendroth. By permission of the author.

Grahn, Judy. "They say she is veiled" and "Grand Grand Mother is returning" from *The Queen Of Wands*. © 1982 by Judy Grahn. By permission of the author.

Griffin, Susan. "Our Mother" from *Bending Home: Selected and New Poems*. © 1998 by Susan Griffin. Reprinted by permission of Copper Canyon Press, P.O. Box 271, Port Townsend, WA 93868.

Hadewijch II. "You who want knowledge" from *Women in Praise of the Sacred*, edited by Jane Hirshfield. © 1994 by Jane Hirshfield. HarperCollins Publishers, N.Y.

H.D. From "Tribute to the Angels" from *Collected Poems, 1912–1944*. Copyright © 1982 by The Estate of Hilda Doolittle. Reprinted by permission of New Directions Publishing and Carcanet Press, Manchester, England.

Harvey, Andrew. "A Prayer to the Divine Mother" from *The Return of the Mother*. Copyright © 1995 by Andrew Harvey. Reprinted with permission of Frog, Limited, Berkeley, California.

Hildebrandt, Ziporah. "In Hecate's Garden," "Persephone," and "Kali" © 1998 by Ziporah Hildebrandt. By permission of the author.

Hinckley, Priscilla Baird. "The New Our Father" © 1995 by Priscilla Hinckley. By permission of the author.

Hixon, Lex. "Who can keep a blazing fire tied in a cotton cloth?" and "My blissful Mother exists fully through every creature!" from *Mother of the Universe*. © 1994 by Lex Hixon. Quest Books, Wheaton, Ill. By permission of the publisher.

Hollander, Vicki. "Rosh Chodesh Tishrei" © 1998 by Vicki Hollander. By permission of the author.

Homer. "Hymn to Aphrodite" (from *The Homeric Hymns*) from *The Goddess Companion*, forthcoming from Llewellyn Publications. © 1998 by Patricia Monaghan. By permission of the author. "The Hymn to the Earth," and excerpts from "The Hymn to Hestia," and "The Hymn to the Moon" from *The Homeric Hymns*, translated by Charles Boer. Spring Publications. © 1970. Eighth printing 1996. Woodstock, Conn.

Roberts, Teresa Noelle. "Apotheosis of the Kitchen Goddess II," from *Cries of the Spirit,* ed. by Marilyn Sewell. Beacon Press. © 1991.

Rupp, Joyce. "Sophia" from *The Star in My Heart.* © 1990 by Joyce Rupp. Innisfree Press. By permission of Innisfree Press.

Sanchez, Carol Lee. "Corn Children" from *A Mountain Climber's Handbook* by Carol Lee Sanchez. © 1985 by Carol Lee Sanchez. By permission of the author.

Sappho. "In the young spring evening," translated by Charoula. © 1994 by Charoula. By permission of the translator. "It's no use" and "Prayer to my lady of Paphos" excerpted from *Sappho: A New Translation,* translated by Mary Barnard. University of California Press. © 1958 by The Regents of the University of California; © renewed 1984 by Mary Barnard. By permission of University of California Press.

Sarton, May. "The Invocation to Kali " copyright © 1971 by May Sarton. "The Muse as Medusa," copyright © 1971 by May Sarton. From *Selected Poems by May Sarton,* ed. Serena Sue Hilsinger and Lois Brynes. Reprinted by permission of W. W. Norton & Company. "When a woman feels alone" from *Letters from Maine* by May Sarton. Copyright © 1984 by May Sarton. Reprinted by permission of W. W. Norton. The poems "The Invocation to Kali" and "When a woman feels alone" reprinted from *Coming into Eighty* by May Sarton, published in Great Britain by The Women's Press, © 1995, 34 Great Sutton Street, London, EC1V ODX, is used by permission of The Women's Press.

Shange, Ntozake. "We Need a God Who Bleeds Now" © 1983 by Ntozake Shange. From *A Daughter's Geography* by Ntozake Shange. Reprinted by permission of St. Martin's Press and by the permission of Russell & Volkening as agents for the author.

Shikibu, Izumi. "Watching the moon" from *The Ink Dark Moon,* translated by Jane Hirshfield with Mariko Aratani. Copyright © 1990 by Jane Hirshfield and Mariko Aratani. Reprinted by permission of Vintage Books, a division of Random House.

Simon, Leslie. "Kali" © 1998 by Leslie Simon. By permission of the author.

Sornberger, Judith. "When She Laughs" © 1995 by Judith Sornberger. By permission of the author.

Starhawk. "Demeter's Song." Words and music © 1992 by Starhawk. From the audiotape *Let It Begin Now* by Reclaiming Collective. Serpentine Music, P.O. Box 2564, Sebastopol, CA 95473. By permission of the author.

Taggard, Genevieve. "Demeter," from *Slow Music,* by Genevieve Taggard, copyright © 1946, renewed 1974, published by Harper & Brothers. Reprinted by permission of Marcia D. Liles.

Valiente, Doreen. "The Charge of the Goddess." Starhawk adaptation. © 1956 by Doreen Valiente. By permission of Robert Hale.

Villanueva, Alma Luz. "From the Healing Dark," "The Planet Earth Speaks" from *Planet,* © 1993 by Alma Luz Villanueva. Bilingual Press. "Song of the Self: The Grandmother" from *Life Span,* © 1984 by Alma Luz Villanueva. Place of Herons Press. By permission of the author.

Winter, Miriam Therese. "In the beginning" from *The Gospel According to Mary.* © 1993 by Miriam Therese Winter. Crossroad Publishing, N.Y. By permission of Crossroad Publishing.

Wisdom of Solomon 6:12–16. Scripture taken from *Today's English Version,* second edition, copyright © 1992 by American Bible Association. Used by permission.

Wolkstein, Diane, and Samuel Noah Kramer. Excerpts from *Inanna, Queen of Heaven and Earth.* © 1983 by Diane Wolkstein and S. Noah Kramer. Harper & Row Publishers. By permission of Diane Wolkstein.

Young, Irene. "A Mermaid Knows" and "Visit to the Palace of Venus." © 1998 by Irene Young. Reprinted by permission of the author.

INDEX OF FIRST LINES